<u>**ABOUT THIS BOOK**</u>

This is the story of a misfit, a reluctant British conscript of World War II who found solace during two years of tribulation in the armed forces and its aftermath by writing letters to an American friend in a somewhat similar predictament. The mood of this authentic human document varies from elation to utter dejection as the young soldier attempts with almost total ineptitude to deal with the incompatible situation in which he finds himself. Yet this is no despairing tale of self-pity. On the contrary, the key-note is an ebullient humour — a sense of the absurd, the over-all picture that of ludicrous comedy even farce. Yet farce with a serious dimension ever-present which belies the often fatuous style in which the writer expresses himself.

This then is more than plain autobiography — the edited scribbled letters of a precocious youth, it is a denigration, not only of the institutions of war, but of the nature of those who wage war (by implication, on both sides of the conflict).

# DEAR COURTNEY
## OR
## WHY I NEVER WON THE D.S.O.

Graham Lewis

*Illustrated by the Author*

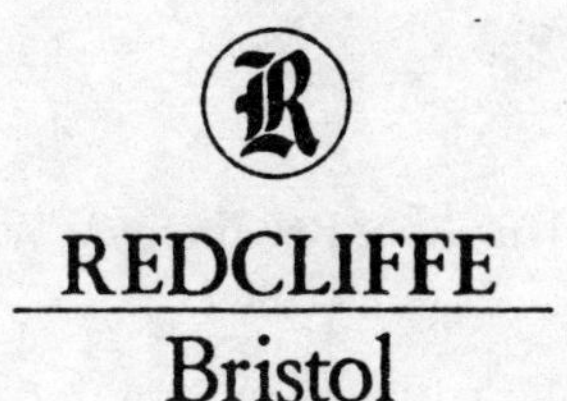

REDCLIFFE

Bristol

First published 1985 by Redcliffe Press Ltd.
49 Park Street, Bristol



Printed and bound in Great Britain by A. Wheaton & Co. Ltd.,
Exeter

ISBN 0 948265 30 2

# PREFACE

The following text is copied from actual letters, written 1943–8, and is fact not fiction. My thanks to Courtney for keeping each and every one over the years. His replies, I regret to say, have been lost.

G.L. 1985

Life is a jest, and all things show it;
I thought so once, but now I know it.

*John Gay*

# PART ONE

Dear Courtney,

This is my third letter. Not number 1, nor number 2, but number 3. Number 1 was scrawled in pencil, number 2 accompanied my latest and best contribution to our mutual short-story, and this, as I say, is number 3.

Courtney, old lad, if you ever see a sailor waving a flag on a battleship you'll know it's me — or one of the thousands of other signalmen employed in the Royal Navy! Yes, I took my medical yesterday (P.G.W's birthday) and passed A.1. It could have been B.1. or C.1. but it was A.1. The medical, incidentally, was a sort of farce. You spent four hours messing around with a lot of old men disporting themselves as doctors, and missed your lunch! They'd look at your teeth and check your eye-sight as o.k. There was one miserable chap there who was deaf in both ears and suffered from foot-and-mouth disease. They put him in A.2. Actually I think the B group is reserved for all applicants in iron lungs. And I suppose when they want recruits for C group they go round yelling, 'Bring out your dead!'

But joking apart Courtney, I thought I'd enter as a signalman because I shall learn semaphore and morse, both of which, I think you'll agree, might be useful in later life! I doubt whether I shall be called up before my eighteenth birthday which is on December 9th, but as the man uttered so enigmatically, 'You never know, do you?' So when you receive this letter I shall probably have been in the service a month or two! This is one reason why I want your part of the story as soon as possible. I won't have time to type stories in the navy, although I chose it in preference as I thought I might have some spare time during those salubrious hours at sea while the U-boats are waiting to strike!

Well, old tack in the tyre, I must terminate. I suppose the proper thing is to send kind regards to Mop and Pop. So here they are: one for Pop and one for Mop. And if you are so injudicious as to read this aloud to the assembled family, be sure to give a long pause after the funny bits to give 'Meatball' a sporting chance!

Au revoir,

Graham

November 6th 1943

Dear Courtney,

You ought to have got the short-story by the time you read this. Hurry up and return it. I expect your part to reach me by the middle of December, if I'm still here. And I doubt whether I'll get the long brown envelope with 'On His Majesty's Service' emblazoned in large type across the top before my birthday which is December 9th.

Every morning I bounce hopefully downstairs to see if your dashed story's arrived. Of course there is always a latent fear that the long brown envelope might be reclining on the salver. All hopes are usually dashed to the ground when I spot a letter from Peter which usually reads: 'Dear Graham. Nothing much going on here at school. Love, Pete. P.S. Please send my cricket bat, my green stamp album, my ear-muffs, which are probably at the bottom of the large trunk in the cellar. (You will find the key for this in that box of old keys in the attic.) And please buy me a yo-yo. P.P.S. You don't mind, do you?'

The only item worthy of mention among recent events is my visit to see my great aunt Minnie who eeks out a frugal livelihood by the somewhat superior method of owning a prosperous weaving mill. The result is that she is simply rolling in the stuff, and a useful aunt to have around. Aunt

2

Minnie is a cheerful old soul, simply exuding altruism. She meets one on the doorstep of the old homestead with a blast of the old voice, which sounds something like Snozzle Durante with bronchial asthma. She then embraces you heartily on both cheeks (I always have to bring a large-size bottle of after-shaving lotion along), and charges upstairs with the intention of dispensing gooseberry jam and other goodies in your direction. She is also a confirmed jig-saw puzzle addict.

As I say, this trip of mine is the only thing worth mentioning at present, so as there is nothing else to write about the logical thing to do is close.

Au rev,

Graham

December 14th 1943

Dear Courtney,

Your second letter, with the story, has come at last. It took five weeks and three days to cross. Thanks for the photos which are very good likenesses, especially that one, 'On the wings of Thought'.

First, I must just give you a pointer about fixing the U.S. postage stamp. I am not sure what sort it was; whether it was one of those purple ones featuring a tired-looking eagle with Win The War embellished across it, or whether it was a stamp of utterly different design. You see, old lad, it had completely detached itself during the journey. I also recall that another stamp impinged on your first letter arrived hanging languidly by its left ear. So give the next one a good lick, won't you?

To turn to the story. You say that you need me to smooth out your 'indigestible hunks of literature'. This was certainly one of them! A prize specimen. I'm not saying it wasn't good stuff: it was. But the spelling!, the grammar!, and the writing!!! It almost needed to be decoded. However, my great brain asserted itself as usual, and here is the result. Your main stuff, of course, was about Hank opening the drawer in Carbacker's study, so it all had to be re-written. However, the whole of that passage had an amusing yet unforced quality which shows we are improving. The part I like best is that bit: 'He felt rather than saw a foreign presence in the darkness. He felt it still more when a hard and no doubt blunt instrument struck him on the base of the skull, and he pitched forward unconscious.'

Well, Courtney, I admit I was sort of hoping you would suggest we collaborate on another story, in fact I have been working on a new idea myself. It has not yet taken tangible form but I can tell you it concerns a scrap-salvage campaign at the school. I am introducing a new character — the champion ear-wiggler of Aaron Burr Co-ed, and I will be sending you the full scenario and first instalment shortly.

I send all my heart-felt commiserations on your recent promotion from Whitehead to Payne. Believe me, I understand. She once taught me history; 4A, I think it was. Anyway, we didn't see eye-to-eye on the Civil War. I said Sherman should not have marched, and she said he should have. The result was disastrous. I delivered an ultimatum: I said that unless she admitted that Sherman was a damn fool and should have known better than to march about all over the place, I would chuck in the old history book, and never whiten her blackboard again. Which was precisely what I did. To show her how strong my feelings were I believe I took up Home Economics under 'Stinky' Davies! Such is life, Courtney. The moral is: blush unseen when you get to Sherman's march.

Incidentally, Aunt Minnie, whom I mentioned in one of my previous epistles, has come to a bitter end. Dying of double-pneumonia, she leaves a textile mill with joint estate and a large cupboard of gooseberry jam. In these parlous days of malnutrition I think I'd prefer the gooseberry jam. My mother, who was suffering from a headache that day, sent me off to purchase a wreath. This I did, and wrote a card to identify the sender. I thought it was rather a good effort but Mother apparently did not. She sent frantic telegrams all over England in an abortive attempt to intercept it. A stiff critic might call it unconventional but no one, I should have thought, would have used the adjective Mother selected which was 'Terrible!' Written suitably in purple ink, it ran: 'Compassionate consolations and commiserations to each and everyone concerned in this irremediable disaster. Yours, the Lewis family.' Judge for yourself, Courtney.

Time is marching on with substantial strides and still I've heard nothing from the Navy. I expect to any day now, though. Will wire you when I do.

P.S. I trust little Meatball is well and taking his Bile Beans.

March 28th 1944

Dear Courtney,

The inevitable has happened and a week on Thursday (April 6th) I proceed to Skegness in Yorkshire where I shall board some blighted frigate by the name of H.M.S. Royal Arthur to take my preliminary training. I have just learnt that I should have entered through some vague system known enigmatically as the Y Scheme. However my interest in such proceedings is non-existent: Y Scheme or Z Scheme, no one realizes better than I do that I am walking into a nightmare.

Doubtless you are thinking that this letter is infused with despondency; however, Courtney, the truth is that the papers arrived at an infelicitous moment. For one thing I had just got your letter telling me of your own imminent induction into the forces. Ghastly! I thought I was the sole fish to be caught in the net. For another, I have just caught an outsize in common colds through riding about on top of a motor car in a high wind.

In view of the impending disaster, I fear I may not be

able to find time to work on our two short-stories in the coming weeks as I believe they keep you pretty hard at it scrubbing decks. However, I am going to work assiduously these few remaining days, and attempt to complete Part 2 of your story before I go.

Time is pressing so I must close.

P.S. Keep writing here till informed to the contrary.

May 10th 1944

Dear Courtney,

After three weeks of hell at Skegness, I have moved to this camp for training.

Before I make some choice remarks about life in the King's Navy, I will devote a few lines to our necessarily neglected story writing. There is some superb material here, and if only circumstances were favourable I could produce some first-rate stuff: the fatuous gas-mask drill at once springs to mind. I can envisage Cosmo and Hank running amok amidst the blister gas! However, for the time being these things cannot be as from six in the morn till eight in the eve Ordinary (?) Signalman Lewis is sorely tried, and only occasionally does he ~~find a brief~~ moment for writing. As for drawing; I have only had the chance to make one rough caricature, and this in the back of my pay-book!

As I say, there is loads of promising material here, Courtney, and to give you a glimpse of life on H.M.S. Ganges (a training ship since 1806) I cannot do better than list a few samples.

The first thing to strike you on reaching the place is that it isn't a ship at all. True, it has a two-hundred foot mast complete with full rigging, and people keep referring to things being 'abaft the fo'xle' and so forth; but the fact remains that it isn't a ship but a barracks. The next thing to strike you like a blow from a marline-spike are the number of effigies of Horatio Nelson that adorn the establishment:

decorative perhaps, but one can go too far. If they had one of Nelson and one of Hawkins and one of that sea-dog who fought off the Spanish Armada, it might be tolerable; but despite the rather fetching likeness of Boadicia(?) on the front gate, the general effect is one of monotony.

The next thing to forcibly strike the raw recruit is the Royal Navy's addiction to the 'march past'; his life, in fact, is almost a continual 'march past'. To be fair, there is the occasional P.T. session to break the monotony; there was one this afternoon. As usual we were greeted by a bouncing bunch of muscle men known as 'gut bashers'. They prance in flexing their biceps, and after performing one or two preliminary hand-springs, they cheerfully tell you to thump the next man vigorously in the vitals. Then when you both stagger back — physical wrecks, they start you off on the sideways-and-upwards-stretch. This is not to be confused with the sideways-and-upwards-stretch that we all know as everyone is compelled to sing 'She'll Be Coming Down The Mountain' at the same time. I'm sure you will sympathize with me when I tell you I started to bellow 'Who's Afraid Of The Big Bad Wolf' after the first verse! We ought to have a gym instructor in our next story, Courtney. I visualize a short muscular Swede: once a tubercular case, but now a fully-fledged keep-fit addict who eats grass, etc. Think about it, Courtney, but be sure to give him a one-track mind.

I don't know how you are getting along though I imagine you are going through pretty much the same kind of hell as I am. This place is positively rife with insanity. If they're not a bunch of idiots of the 'wart-hog' category, then they're the other sort of lunatic — 'empire-builders'. Few, if any, misfits, and frankly I am feeling the strain. I have acquired a sort of vapid comatose expression and go through the day's programme like a zombie, disconcerted by nothing.

Will finish this later.

*May 13th 1944*

Please excuse the writing, but I am surrounded by a

crowd of Leading Seamen ingurgitating beer! Incidentally, old lad, I don't think I told you that I was pronounced colour blind by a squad of doctors, and was thereafter discounted from the executive commission. (Greens and blues, you know. They flashed a light which I said was a bluey green, whereas the squad insisted it was a greeny blue!) A real stroke of luck — this, as my chances of lasting the course, I have since discovered, were as negligible as a sailor's soap ration. At present I am going for a commission in the 'special' branch. Having now passed various elementary tests along with the ordinary seamen, I graduate to another sphere and, if lucky, I will qualify as an officer in some specialized capacity. I say 'if lucky' as they only need a minimum of commissioned officers at the present time. Anyway, don't be surprised if I end up as the special officer in charge of the ship's cat!

I have come to the conclusion, by the way, that the Navy is nothing but a slave racket. The first week, all I did was fire-watch from 4 a.m.; the second, I swept roads all day; the third, I enacted the duties of cook, which in fact are those of dish-washer and floor-waxer. Currently I am working, under considerable strain, as offal-man. At the close of each meal I don blue overalls, grab a bucket, and collect all the crusts and scraps overlooked by the locusts.

After profound deliberation, Courtney, I have come to the conclusion that, for me, there is only one possible attitude of mind whilst in amongst those who go down to the sea in ships. The alternatives are these: (1) Cast story-writing and all else that matters to the winds, become a stiff-necked blister with a one-track mind and rise to the inspiring rank of rear-admiral. Or, (2) Look upon the whole affair as a sort of unavoidable mistake; accept it as valuable experience yet retain a certain detached indifference towards it. If getting a commission entails comparative disfigurement of the neck leaving no time or energy for anything that matters, then slide surreptitiously out in search of a softer spot. I don't have to tell you which is my point of view: doubtless it is yours also. I frankly admit that I have only put myself in for this commission thing to escape the company of my present bed-fellows. (I am speaking metaphorically, of course!) The thought of gold braid was never an incentive.

Well, old colleague, I must now close. I think I have covered all the ground; all, that is, except to say — I wish the hell you were here! We could burn through this mistaken idea of existence like flames through a wheat field!

P.S. The Leading Seamen having consumed five pints apiece are becoming a trifle obstreperous. They have begun to tie rolling-sheep-bends in my boot laces!

June 11th 1944

Dear Courtney,

Having a brief respite from 'durance vile' I shall use it to compose yet another of my side-splitting missives. My free time these days is almost non-existent, but I'll do my damnedest to scribble a few words once a fortnight.

I have just opened your heart-rending letter posted at the end of April. What can I say, except that I have every confidence in your resilience, and that although you may be badly battered during the process, I am convinced you will take all obstacles in your stride.

With regard to your effusive remarks about this biography of Robert E. Lee; even if I could procure a copy which is extremely unlikely, it would be impossible to find time to read it. Things are so tight that I can barely find five minutes in which to peruse a little Wodehouse. The camp library has made a supreme effort. I found two ancient-looking volumes on a shelf one day, and having blown away the cobwebs, I discovered they were, 'Ukridge' and 'Lord Emsworth and Others'.

Doubtless you would like me to elucidate the reasons for my lack of spare time? Well, the cause of the trouble is that I have now joined the chosen few in the advanced class which means we work unremittingly from 6.30 a.m. to 7 p.m.; and this with barely enough time to consume the necessary sustenance. I must confess I have few hopes of sticking this course, and the chances are that my cylinders will start to misfire shortly. So if my next letter begins: 'Dear Marmaduke, The onions are coming along splendidly. How is Aunt Priscilla?' just shake your head sadly and murmur, 'Poor Graham! Such is war.'

But the conviction grows, old lad, that you and I are the only sane individuals in a seething mass of lunacy. The general atmosphere of this place is the incessant expulsion of energy. Everyone from the admiral downwards strides past you with a purposeful step as if he had a bare two minutes to man the guns. In fact he is probably off to fetch another bottle of boot cleaner! What I am getting at is that there is always something to be done and not enough time to do it in, so that only occasionally does the mind come to the surface for brief interludes of thought and elevating reading. To put it in a nutshell, Courtney, I am gradually becoming intolerably bored with the entire deluded existence here. So don't be surprised if you pick up a newspaper one fine day to be confronted by the disquieting headline: 'MARLINE-SPIKE MURDERER CLAIMS SIXTH VICTIM. Admiral Found Pinned To Yard Arm During Dog Watch'.

The first phase of the course I am taking finishes in two weeks time. If I'm to get some leave (and the Royal Navy is about as tight on leave as a corset would be on Eugene Pallette) I'll get it then. If they still consider G.L. as a suitable officer candidate, I will then embark on the second phase of my training which may well involve a few strenuous weeks at sea scrubbing decks.

Next week sees a string of exams finishing up with a Commander's Board. The gist of this is that you enter a room packed to bursting point with the Commander (a fat chap) and a bevy of psychologists who glare at you from beneath forbidding eye-brows. If you happen to tickle your left ear, the psychologists scribble notes on bits of paper reading, 'Nervous inclination — perhaps afraid of fire?' In short, it's a personality check-up. There is, let's admit it, a strong possibility that the Commander and his men may not consider G.L. to be the required officer personality, in which case I will notify you as expeditiously as possible.

I am competing, of course, with some of the most dyed-in-the-wool young empire-builders; men who will doubtless all die gloriously and as a result get their photographs printed in the Daily Sketch. My point of view is this: if G.L. does not meet their requirements, then they either revise their requirements or they do not get G.L. Egotistical, you think? All right, but without this attitude my independent spirit would long ago have been annihilated. I speak candidly, Courtney, to give you a clear understanding of things; things of more importance than any frivolous anecdotes describing how I learnt to 'cat the anchor'!

I suppose no true and unswerving supporter of the Allied Nations' cause should complete a letter at this time without mentioning the Normandy invasion. So there it is, duly mentioned: it's a subject which does not inspire anything witty in the observation line.

P.S. I want you to know: in moments of stress I always chew one of your esteemed toothpicks!

*July 16th 1944*

What-ho, Courtney old sausage!

Excuse me for beginning in such a repulsive manner, old horse, but I'm actually on leave! Yes, the Navy has condescended to come across with severn days: severn blissful days of civilization. Don't waste any space in your next letter disparaging my spelling of the word 'seven', old boy, as your remarks would be entirely wasted. The fact is that on such a day as this it is quite conceivable that, given the opportunity, I could spell pusillanimous p-u-z-z-i-l-a-n-i-m-u-z without turning a hair.

Despite a rigorous course in morse and many tedious hours spent practising semaphore, you will notice that my typing is as good as ever, if not better. Yet I haven't heard so much as the click of a typewriter for over 14 weeks. The

Navy, Courtney, has not changed me a bit. So far my personality has proved impervious to the storm. It is a glorious day and I am off to have tea on the veranda. Will bring you back a bun. . .

(Some hours later)

I have just finished a strenuous round of croquet; an exasperating game. All I needed was one to win and I thought I had it in the bag. But something went wrong with the wrist-work, and my ball, having tacked down the lawn like a dipping-lug cutter in a fresh wind, came to rest in a bed of delphiniums leaving my mother an easy 60 foot shot to win the game! I have taken a number of snap-shots this afternoon, including a view of the house itself resplendent in the glories of summer. If they come out (they were supposed to have been developed before 1933) I will send with my next.

Your last two letters arrived together on July 8th. One was postmarked May 8th and the other May 16th. Both were very amusing and full of information.

You discourse at great length, old lad, on my proclivities as a 'test passer'. Don't grieve, Courtney, but your illusions are about to be irreparably shattered. In short, I have to tell you that I failed this commission business completely and utterly. How right you were when you said that I was psychologically unsuited for this mundane realism. From the first my interest was elsewhere. When I should have been learning the rudiments about lowering a sea-boat I was preoccupied putting the finishing touches to a caricature of the worthy instructor. When I was supposed to be drinking in the intricacies of Robinson's Disengaging Gear I was in fact composing a satirical sketch of the vagaries of Leading Seamen. When the exams came along I knew far less than the rest of my contingent, and was not even worried about it. Even so, my luck held good and I bluffed my way through to make 84 in Gunnery and 76 in Seamanship!!

By this time, however, I knew for certain that the thing

wasn't for me: the game was just not worth the proverbial candle. So when that mystical rite known as the Commander's Board eventually hove in sight, I simply decided not to play along with it. In short, I decided to present myself before the board as G.L. with no disguises.

The correct seamanlike way to approach this Board business is as follows. . . A bell is sounded, and the aspiring sub-lieutenant who has been waiting in a state of trepidation outside the door mutters a silent prayer and goose-steps in. He is momentarily paralysed by a sea of piercing eyes which glare at him from all sides but he retains the stiff upper lip. At length he singles out the Commander who is gazing at him steadily. Under this devastating scrutiny he begins to suspect that he is wearing a droopy lanyard, but he dare not drop his eyes to verify this as he realizes instinctively that the success or failure of the interview depends on whether he can maintain an unflinching stare into the eye-ball of the god-like being opposite. For the next five minutes he continues to gaze steadily and unblinkingly until almost pop-eyed.

"Number?" barks the demi-god at last.

"JX 61666, sir!" retorts our pimply candidate clicking his heels. Eyebrows on both the port and starboard are now twitching and there is much scribbling on scraps of paper.

"And what is your ambition in His Majesty's Royal Navy?" barks the demi-god.

Our candidate gives of his best.

"To sink a German battleship, sir," he answers smartly.

"Very good JX 61666. You may go. . . Call JX 61667."

Our candidate makes a half-right turn and goose-steps out.

From this short sketch it will not surprise you to hear that when it came to my turn, I must have cut rather an incongruous figure; 'lackadaisical' is the word that springs to mind. I regret to say, old lad, I never even mentioned sinking a German battleship. I made it pretty clear that my main reason for wanting a commission was to escape from the

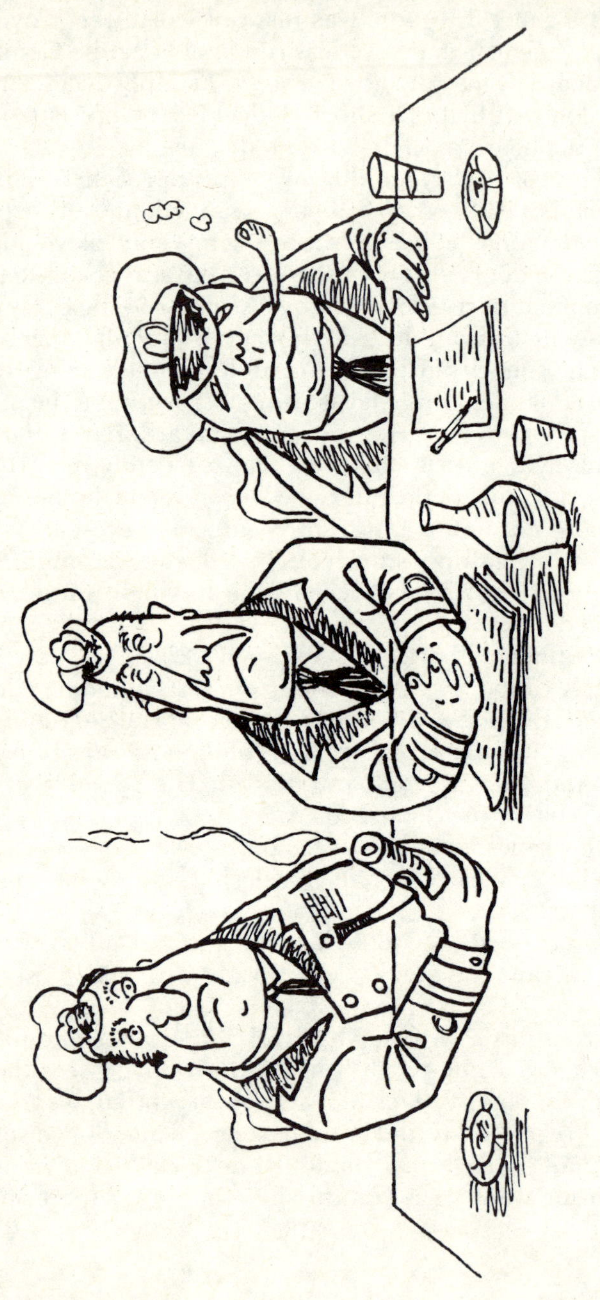

wart-hogs on the lower deck — in fact to live as comfortably as possible until I can get out altogether! When I left the Commander's presence all the eyebrows were looking pretty deprecating, I can tell you.

The other Sunday, the chaplain was expounding some sound views on how easy it is to become mentally pusillanimous while in a routined and organized world like the Navy. Every minute of your day is planned, and you are regulated like an automaton so that there is no chance for the individual to assert his initiative. How true! Beware of this, Courtney, and read your Wodehouse daily. (Actually the chaplain recommended the bible.) Try a spot of writing on your next leave. The reason I failed the c.w. course was simply because I esteemed my mental health to be more important than an obsession with things nautical.

Some days later. Sunday 23rd to be exact.

Well, old fly in the sauce, the leave is over, and here I am back at Ganges awaiting transfer to Skegness to be recategoried. I shall have a shot at 'writer': keeping books, a sedentary job! I shall keep you informed of all future developments when things are less hazy. I must say I feel very relieved at having given up this commission business; it's like walking out of a hot engine room. I hope you will decide to do likewise. Try and get some humble pursuit like 'telescope polisher' — it's the only way!

Just heard I leave tomorrow (6 a.m.) for Skegness.

Yours, with my head in the proverbial clouds,

*August 13th 1944*

Dear Courtney,

Since my last missive stirring things have been happening, not least that to all intents and purposes I am no longer in the Navy. To explain: on reaching Skegness I was tersely informed that, not being a volunteer for the Navy, I was to be transferred into the Army. Upon receipt of this shattering news I made a number of calls on any admirals I could find, sparing no pains to make the point clear that I resented this transfer business to the point of anathema. As I write, the whole thing is still in the air, and I don't know what will happen next.

There is no point in my wasting space trying to sketch out my future: in the Navy nothing is certain, and I cross stiles as I come to them. I just keep plodding along awaiting my day of emancipation. Hitler and his gang appear to be more or less a spent force now, and by and large England is permeated with an airy optimism believing that the end is not far distant.

At the moment, I am employed as an acting coal-heaver, stevedore, bottle-washer, and general maid-of-all-work. Quite a come-down from my c.w. activities! This week I temporarily take office as a tiller of the soil. I have been placed in charge of seven fellow tillers, and together we shall encourage the growth of onions at some nearby farm. I am now a mere Ordinary Seaman and have put myself down for RADAR (wireless location). This involves a two month course on the Isle of Man, after which I would join a ship. Who knows, I could dock at Norfolk, Va., yet, though the Fiji Isles are more of a probability.

To end this hasty letter, a brief word on current entertainment. I caught up with 'The Adventures of Robin Hood' last week: been watching for this show for four years. A colourful pageant, very appealing to my starved imagination. One of the effects of the war is that the swashbuckling adventurers of bygone days have been replaced by hoards of jack-booted Nazis. Give me the swashbuckler every time, for despite a tendency to punctuate his speech with such ejaculations as 'Hot Dawg!', the setting is a lot less depressing than the forbidding block-houses which surround the whipping-post in the other type of film. Also, I have just finished perusing an interesting book on 'The Art of Walt Disney'. It confirms my belief that he is a true artist in every sense of the word.

P.S. To answer your query about doodle-bugs*: they flit higher and thither like bees in the summer sunshine.

August 19th 1944

Dear Courtney,

I think I'll make this letter a series of disconnected impressions. I can see I shall have no time for anything else from now on. I've got to start once more at the bottom and pull my way up to a condition of comparative stability.

Yesterday I sent you a succinct cable appraising you of the facts, and now I am on my way, thoroughly dejected, to join the Territorial Army. What an anniversary of our separation!

I am scribbling this on an antiquated train. The atmosphere is none too good as I am packed in with the most deplorable brood of vituperating wart-hogs imaginable! The train seems to be uncertain of its destination at the moment. It can't make up its mind whether to go backwards or forwards. The wart-hogs think it's all great fun and are whistling at passing females. One of them has just announced with a great deal of spirit that, as far as he is concerned, he'll take anything between nine and ninety!

The one compensation in the whole deplorable affair is that the transit camp we are headed for is at (*censored*), so home is within easy reach. . . Just passed through Sheffield. A grimy-looking spot: could do with a good clean! Will continue anon. Must look for sustenance.

Friday, August 25th 1944

I am lying full-length in the bottom of a lifeboat in the bows of the S.S. Something-or-other anchored just off (*censored*). I get kicked around, don't I! Courtney, old barracuda, I am in one hell of a spot! Graham Lewis is being tried as never before. At (*censored*) we were thrown into khaki

*V1 rockets

17

without any discrimination whatever. Along with the other dregs from the Navy and Air Force I have been press-ganged into the (*censored*) Regiment. Then, before we had time to turn round, we were bundled like cattle on board this damnable troop ship. And here I am incarcerated with the vilest wart-hogs condemned to six weeks route-marching, grenade-throwing, and bayonet-sticking in their intelligent company! Do you blame me, Courtney, when I tell you I have tried to volunteer for the coal mines! At the moment my equilibrium is in grave jeopardy: this is the last straw!

Well, I won't go on pitying myself, but it's a plight I wouldn't have deemed it possible to get into. (So much cannon fodder.) The chances of this mining scheme coming off are slight, and though I know it would be Hell, I think the chances of maintaining my sanity would be less remote than in my present situation. It is a well-known fact that infantry training entails squashing all individualism in a character to make him into a pig-sticking automaton. I'm in a state of mental desperation, old lad. Can G.L.'s sanity survive such a process, that's what I'm worried about. These insects I'm with are hardly human; they have no minds, only instincts. Their language is unutterably foul.

Out of two thousand, there is only one chap whom I can talk to. We have both volunteered for the mines but I am bound to admit, it looks hopeless. My only real hope is a quick end to this war.

Well, old boy, enough brooding on this ghastly state of affairs for the time being: I will elaborate later when I get to this Hell hole.


*Sunday, August 27th 1944*

Well, Courtney old horse,

The aforementioned Hell hole has now materialized and I am writing this passage in one of the irrepressible NAAFI canteens which seem to infest all camps, whether Navy, Army, or Air Force. From Belfast, I was lugged off into the heart of the glowing Irish countryside; the locomotive responsible reminding me very much of a child's clockwork toy. The thing was so small and was working under such a strain that large pink flames were emanating from the funnel and other odd spots. I got a fleeting impression of Belfast; a city untroubledby the rush and bustle of business enterprise. A somnolent city, I would call it, now that the I.R.A. — the chaps who drop bombs into pillar boxes — have gone to ground.

Well, old boy, they seem to have sold the last iced bun for the evening and are shutting up shop, so I had better discontinue. I commence the 18 week course tomorrow.

Tuesday, August 29th 1944

Last night I managed to get into the camp's cinema-cum-gymnasium to see 'Jane Eyre'. (You watch the show hanging from a rope: the shilling tickets are allowed to hold onto th wall-bars.) I suppose it might be loosely called a good film, but for me it totally failed to click. Orson Welles' acting is, like his personality, preposterous. He emphatically refuses to appear until he is furnished with a cloak, a gloomy castle, and a few flashes of lightning. What I did relish in this highly melodramatic film was the reassurance it gave me that the finer emotions still exist even while I flounder in this unreal nightmare. Frankly, old lad, this current programme is insupportable. I could just about tolerate the Navy but not my predicament now. I need hardly tell you that psychologi-cally I am totally unfit for this outfit. Put yourself in my position and imagine how you would react. I can't go into it here in any detail as our letters are censored and I should indubitably be hauled before some colonel or other charged with sedition, sabotage, or what-not. This, of course, is one of my chief objections to the set-up: any sort of protest is immediately annihilated. No individualism: you even have to make your beds identically! However, old lad, you may rest assured that whatever the impending physical and mental torments, they will fail in their efforts to turn me into the conventional pig-sticking automaton!

Today they issued me with a foul great gun equipped with a repellent pig-sticker — presumably for impaling Japs, though I use it for paring my finger-nails. You will see from the sketch below that G.L. is even more of a misfit here than he was in the R.N.

I enclose a photo taken on leave showing me browsing through the Sunday Pictorial for 'corn'. Also, my greatest find of the year: a picture — though a poor one — of the ineffable P.G.W. The accompanying para. is only enclosed to show how some people unerringly get hold of the wrong end of the stick.

Will write again soon.

**On the last page of this letter, the censor had written: 'Sept. 5. Sorry late postage — Censor.' And I can only assume that it had been subjected to further scrutiny during the intervening seven days. I do know that the censor (the Company Officer) called me into his presence, and indicating my pencilled pages, hazarded the remark: 'I don't think you like the Army much, do you?' I suspect that the letter was instrumental in obtaining my subsequent merciful release from this outfit. G.L. 1985**

*October 4th 1944*

Dear Courtney,

I realize this letter is overdue, but Time has been exceeding the speed limit lately and I have rarely been able to find a moment to fasten the odd boot lace, never mind to compose rib-cracking bulletins to eager recipients such as yourself. However, never fear: as long as I avoid breaking my neck through falling into a slit trench or ravelling my vitals around a barbed wire obstacle, you can rest assured that I will keep in touch.

As you will see from the address, I am once more home on leave and taking a well-earned rest; muscular exertions being confined to wielding cutlery, tickling dogs, and — pulling chains!

In the first place, old lad, I should like to acknowledge the brace of Bulldog Drummond books which made a belated appearance on September 2nd. I cannot be sure when they were dispatched as the parcel seems to have changed its wrapping more than once. Anyway, thanks, old boy, my collection of Bulldog Ds is now complete.

Presumably you have heard the latest on P.G.W.? Following his fall into Allied hands in Paris, he seems to be having inordinate difficulty in reinstating himself with the British. My bone-headed countrymen are sticking to their belief that he is a traitor with characteristic tenacity, and his future is uncertain. He has written three novels and a number of short-stories during his internment, which to me is irrevocable proof that he has preserved his sanity.

Well, old lad, to get down to brass tacks. You are, I am sure, agog to hear my considered observations on the British Territorial Army. My correspondence from camp will have to be somewhat restrained as I found out the hard way that our own officers act as censors. For the moment, however, I can express myself freely!

First, a few facts. I have been conscripted into the Royal Warwicks, regardless of my personal feelings about the infantry. After 12 more weeks training I shall join a unit; so I could end up in a slit trench in Burma, or at best, as a military policeman in Dusseldorf! Am I gripping you? To continue. . . During the journey from Skegness to Huyton Army Transit Camp 'C', Private Graham Lewis might have appeared a trifle despondent to the detached observer. Even the prospect of a cup of tea in the station canteen at Manchester failed to elate him, so it was with a preoccupied air that he sat down at a table, splashing most of his beverage onto the lap of the recruit in the next chair. Such were the dramatic circumstances which brought him face to face with the individual who was destined to be his bosom companion for the next two months.

This individual, whose name is Desmond, struck me at once as being a prize specimen of a misfit; almost as much of a fish out of water as myself. And so he proved. His supercilious eyebrow when conversing with N.C.O.s is a sight for sore eyes, while his innocuous, "Oh, I say, sergeant, could you tell me what I have to press next, please?" is as honey from the honeycomb on the Bren Gun range. His view of life can only be called dispassionate. He has a penchant for prunes, and after accumulating vast riches in the ice-cream trade, he intends to while away the rest of his days writing detective fiction. A priceless companion to have around in this predicament, as I am sure you will agree, Courtney: I have actually seen him ask a sergeant-major for a safety pin as his trousers were falling down on parade! I can say without any exaggeration that Desmond and I are the only two of our kind at Camp Ballykinlar, that indelible blot on the landscape where the Mountains of Mourne sweep dolefully down to the sea.

With no exceptions, the rest of the community consists of those two ubiquitous types — the Wart-hog and the Empire-builder, so from the outset Desmond and I were marked men. Those in charge were quick to realize that here was something out of the ordinary, something a little more reluctant to jump through the hoop, and my surmise that the going might prove a trifle sticky was quickly proved correct.

One cannot over-emphasize the fact that the salient intention of infantry training is to break down what vestige of individualism there may be in the unfortunate recruit, and mould him unremittingly into the sort of robot exhibited with David Niven in the film 'The Way Ahead'. (We were marched in to see this film in relays at Huyton.) Naturally, I was on my guard, and it did not surprise me when I was hauled in front of an Army Psychologist of empire-builderish shape and texture within a few days of my arrival.

After staring at me for the best part of five minutes in the hope that I would wilt before such a withering gaze, he suddenly took the initiative.

"You think yourself damned important, don't you?" he barked in a voice like a burst from a Bren gun.

"Frankly, sir," I retorted mildly, "I consider myself the least important soldier in the army: in fact, they'd get along much better without me."

Obviously peppered by this shrapnel he renewed his attack, utilizing the old favourite.

"Who do you mean by 'they'?" he exploded; this time like a mortar bomb.

"Oh, I mean the soldiers, sir."

"You sound as if you despise them!"

I would have liked to have shaken him by the hand for summing things up so exactly: instead I replied languidly,

"I'm sure they are all Grade A pig-stickers, sir, but as bedside companions they leave a lot to be desired."

For some reason this punctured him completely. The last I saw of him, he was sitting, his eyes glazed, drawing handgrenades on the blotting paper!

From then on things moved pretty rapidly for myself and the incomparable Desmond. We avoided our fellow privates, and our fellow privates avoided us. We avoided the corporals, and the corporals avoided us. Sergeants walked by on the other side with a shudder. We came to be known far and wide as the Terrible Twins. An estimable state of affairs, you may say, and so you would be right. The snag was that during working hours the arrangement was not practicable; and more often than not, 'working hours' meant 6 a.m. to 10 at night. My difficulties in adapting myself to the ways of the armed forces invariably emerge during working hours. And the same is true of Desmond. He knows this; I know this; but what can either of us do about it? Sooner or later someone is going to pick up a packet running special excursions from Belfast to watch the Terrible Twins stripping a Bren gun! In fact Desmond, his business brain whirring, is thinking of doing it himself.

So far our training has consisted of a process of inculcation whereby we are taught huge numbers of obvious

facts interspersed by the occasional seven mile race in a thunderstorm wearing boots and a pair of blue shorts. To illustrate the inculcation process, here is an account of a recent lesson in Night Manoeuvres.

One night we were marched into the surrounding wilderness and told to keep our eyes peeled. "Can you see anything?" demands the officer in charge. "Er, no, sir," comes the wary reply. "Very good, very good," says the officer: "there's nothing to see." Somewhat mirth-provoking, you may think? But it was nothing compared to what was to follow. The officer then produced a large whistle and shattered the still of the Irish night with a discordant blast, whereupon two chaps in an adjoining field immediately lit up a couple of gaspers. "Er. . . I can see something now, sir," says one of the brainier lads hesitantly. "What, Hodgkins?" snaps back the officer eagerly. "Two lighted fags, sir," says Hodgkins. "Very good, Hodgkins, very good. And now you know never to smoke cigarettes during night action as they could be seen by the enemy."

The authorities also spend a good deal of time in explaining to us the fallacy of pretending to be a gorse bush in a field of daffodils. But although the subject of camouflage lends itself to satire, I think I shall end by describing another incident which, at the time of going to press, still leads the field by half a furlong.

Picture to yourself the Terrible Twins taking a leisurely saunter through the barracks one fine evening, and ruminating earnestly on this and that. Suddenly there appears on the horizon the life-like replica of the most exaggerated cartoon of a major you can imagine. Desmond did not catch sight of him, whereas I gazed goggle-eyed, all the artist in me brimming with admiration at the spectacle of this perfect archetype. Assuming the worst — that he falls in battle; there is no doubt that the War museum would offer three figures for his red moustache which must be a positive danger on night manoeuvres. In addition to this adjunct, he possessed a pair of steely blue Indian Army eyes which he played on us like a blow-torch. However, it would have taken something more powerful than this to disturb Desmond who was engrossed in his schemes for cornering the lemonade market; so whereas I performed a magnificent salute ending in a sort of shimmer, Desmond merely muttered something about the price of lemon peel after the war. The major — now a veritable conflagration, uttered the word 'Halt!'; and we halted. "Why," he demanded, addressing Desmond, "did you not salute?" "I'm afraid I failed to see you, sir," answered Desmond affably. "You — failed — to — see — me — — —" grunted the officer, flames leaping out of his ears. "You might fail to see a Jap in Burma!" After which portentous pronouncement he strode smartly away!

Enough for one evening, Courtney, enough.


*October 29th 1944*

Dear Courtney,

Despite some blighted woman expounding the mysteries of autumn over the inter-com (which has lately developed a sore throat) and despite a bunch of loud-mouthed wart-hogs exchanging views on this and that, I shall try once again to compose another letter constructed of the usual tangle of laughs and rib-cracking quips.

The last time I wrote you I was recuperating on leave, and I believe I had secreted some hair-raising information within the pages.* You will doubtless be relieved to hear that subsequent developments have rendered this information null and void, and any misgivings you may have felt can now be expunged from your mind. You breathe a sigh of relief? But, laddie, I want you to know I would have perpetrated the deed unquestionably had it not been for the latest vicissitude in events. The true details, the actual machina-

*The code message referred to ran: 'Planning possible bunk. Nothing definite.' Alarming, perhaps, but I need not have worried. Courtney's next letter contained a p.s.: "What does 'bunk' mean?"

tions that were going on in my mind I will not clarify till next
we meet; however, the important thing, Courtney, is that
despite all these misfortunes, the Lewis equilibrium —
though a little shaky — is still rotating on its axis.

What has occurred can be quite simply stated as
follows: I have been transferred from the infantry into the
Royal Army Medical Corps. The news may not surprise you
as by now you must be inured to my erratic movements
However, the more one thinks about it, the more amazing it
seems: the implication being that the authorities have done
something I deemed to be beyond their powers. They have
granted an individual special consideration. Incredible, yet
there it stands! At last being convinced that Private Lewis
was mentally, if not also physically, unsuited to the
pig-sticking programme, they arranged for my *solitary*
transfer to the medical corps, where — though I have no
knowledge of medicine — they considered I would be better
suited. A trifle over-optimistic as things have turned out; the
future looks brighter — yes, but hardly incandescent.

For the next six weeks I shall be stationed here at
Aldershot for yet another bout of basic training, this time
involving Thomas splints, pulmonary arteries, and the like.
The incomparable Desmond, I regret to say, has been left
stranded in the dreadful quagmire at Ballykinlar. I am now
in a branch of the forces that has sound fundamental views
regarding humanity; restorative instead of destructive.
When I trailed in here carrying my rifle it caused quite a
sensation, I can tell you: it was confiscated immediately in
the guard room. Yet when all is said and done, the fact
remains that I am still in the British Territorial Army. As in
Ireland, bone-headed sergeants abound and the wart-hog
remains ubiquitous, though the local variety is less
primitive. In fact, my new comrades are mainly 'old soldiers'
who have seen War and survived to tell the tale. Their
anecdotes are incredibly boring; usually on how they got
bitten by a poisonous spider in Burma. It's surprising how
many got bitten by these spiders — and every bite lethal!
The other element are the mental cases; shell-shock or just

nervous wrecks. Few of these chaps seem to have been bitten by poisonous spiders, but they have a distressing tendency to leap out of bed at 3 a.m. and dance the tango! All in all, it is like a holiday camp after Ballykinlar, though.

For instance, I have just been recruited to the staff of the camp newspaper (readership: 5000) as cartoonist! Not much scope really, but good practice and it will relieve the monotony. I think I'll stir things up a bit with drawings of large bone-headed N.C.O.s! If you don't mind, old boy, I'll hold onto this letter till Thursday when I should be able to enclose a new photo of myself, in Army uniform, and possibly a few specimens from the weekly.

Received the manuscript last Monday. Will not comment here but will iron out and send to my father for typing.

P.S. Although Meatball, dear soul, will have to wait for the time being, I shall personally present him with my Army cap one day!

*November 26th 1944*

Dear Courtney,

I have precisely fifteen minutes in which to dash off this overdue missive as currently I am serving a sentence. Yes, old lad, it will hardly surprise you to hear that your old pal is now a handcuffed criminal! I am on four days c.b.; a farcical experience and one which will probably be repeated before I eventually wander forth into the wide world wearing one of the free-issue civilian suits. My heinous crime is one I would rather not discuss on paper: I was caught leaning up against a wall with my hands in my pockets when I ought to have been listening avidly to a repulsive sergeant explaining the engineering feat of digging a latrine on the field of battle.

As usual I am a marked man because I obviously lack the desired outlook; so naturally the N.C.O.s exercise their authority on my innocent person. Incidentally, a letter from

Desmond tells me he has sunk irremediably into the mire since my departure. Seven charges resulting in an apparently endless sentence have blotted his record.

My course here finishes this week, and I hope to see the last of Boyce Barracks before Christmas. I will try to wangle some leave before — or immediately after the festivities. Think of it, Courtney; Christmas — the time of year when bonhomie reaches its height, and when a partially sane atmosphere descends upon an incorrigible world, and Graham Lewis will probably have to spend it forming fours on a parade ground! I intend to send you something or other for Christmas, however Whitehall (London mixture) is off the list. I have even had minions scouring bomb-torn Whitehall, and their efforts have proved abortive. Their information is that it is a Canadian tobacco and unobtainable here!

You have doubtless watched the ink petering out: I shall continue in pencil. . .

My activities with the camp tabloid have done much to alleviate the oppressive atmosphere of this place. A good deal of the merriment, I should say, was due to the antics of a devil-may-care ex-commando named Wilbur. I have come to the conclusion that the Army is the most sordid institution. My British patriotism, Courtney, which used to irritate you so much — remember? is now a heap of cold ashes. It was an illusion based on ignorance and inflamed by my separation from the Mother Country at such a tender age. I am now, like you, cosmopolitan.

Which brings me to the subject of P.G. Wodehouse. You know, I don't think there is a soul in this country who understands the man: they see him as a sinister-looking cove in a black cloak emblazoned with swastikas! Enclosed are some interesting cuttings bearing on the subject. All this talk about him being 'a British subject'. Typical! Trust the empire-builder to make a political squabble out of it.

The short-story is being typed out and I expect to have it shortly. Upon receipt I shall write a business letter and send to you at once.

Courtney old pickerel!

It is the final day of the Old Year, and being something of a sentimentalist, I have been racking my brains trying to think of a resolution. After careful deliberation I have decided on the following: during 1945, I solemnly resolve to read at least one book not written by P. G. Wodehouse or Sapper. I can almost see your eyes light up as you reach for some brown paper and string and your seven volumes on 'Lee — The Soldier'!

Referring to your latest missive which arrived December 14th; may I say, old lad, that this is one of your best. 'Impregnated with sparkling wit' is a phrase which comes to mind. More about this in a moment.

I expect you are wondering how it is that I am tinkling the keys of the old typewriter? The answer to that one is simple — even childish: having been posted to the military hospital near Chester, I find it not too difficult to traverse the intervening twenty miles at week-ends. A lucky posting, affording a future of revivifying respites! My sojourn at Chester, however, may be brief as I seem to be the only A.1. soldier in the R.A.M.C. For the moment, however, I'm sitting pretty. My duties consist of janitor and general dogsbody to the Opthalmic or Eye Department, including a little sphere and cyl filing (lenses), and the occasional trip to the colonel with monocle repairs (not fictitious). I am making two monocles in my spare moments (one with frame; one without). Will send you the best of these.

The other day I came in to work to be confronted by a bizarre spectacle: a major and two captains lying prostrate in the middle of the corridor trying to see who could do the most push-ups! In case you are curious, I might add that the Eye man, despite his bulk, managed fifteen to the Ear-Nose-and-Throat man's ten. A stout fellah! I have been working a group caricature of everyone in the department, but I'll tear it up and draw another one showing them all doing push-ups!

To revert to your letter. Courtney, your misgivings about Desmond frankly astound me. Although he and I see eye-to-eye on many basic issues, any artistic collaboration with him is simply not on the cards. So forget it. . . And another thing. Frankly, old lad, you strike me as being rather prosaic when you say you see our joint efforts as a means to gaining "a sedentary satisfactory life". Your cartoon idea, I agree, is primarily a money-spinner; but not the stories. Not to me anyhow. Regarding the cartoons: it seems to me the specimens we have sent each other have singularly failed to click. The sort of stuff we have been formulating can be seen on any bookstall, and can be turned out like pop-corn by almost anybody. What they lack is distinction, originality, style. Our ideas are too conventional, too shallow: if we emulate current formulas we are sure to get nowhere. Our drawings (and here I include the joke) should be hall-marked by a style that is instantly recognizable — like a Virgil Partch or an Emett. I only mention this because I think we have both unwittingly hit upon such a style. Hard to put it into words, but it has elements of satire, caricature, and topicality. It is only exemplified in three of the many ideas we have exchanged: (1) your own, 'And Field Marshal Attwood can bring the poker chips ashore.' (2) The gas-mask one: 'Don't shoot till you see the whites of their eyes.' And (3) 'Remember, the signal is the hoot of an owl.' (Unlike my rough sketch, only the eyes of the owls need be visible.) Tell me what you think. Meanwhile I will try and find time to make finished drawings of these three.

P.S. I appreciate your parable of the field of wheat bending with the wind, old horse; but what does the poor old wheat stalk do in the face of a 'twister'? No amount of bending is going to do it any good.

Courtney old lad,

Having an hour at my disposal and the environment being exceptionally salubrious, I shall once more exercise my pen. I am seated in the hospital's spacious billiard room, though my duties are not onerous — hence the missive. In point of fact they consist solely of counting the billiard balls every ten minutes; a precaution, I am told, against the wiles of these mental patients who are apt to try to swallow them, or pocket them, when they think no one is looking. None of the balls look appetizing to me, except perhaps the pink one which I am keeping my eye on.

However, let us dispense with this badinage. You will excuse it I know, being cognizant of my partiality to local colour.

Life at Moston Hall meanders on its merry way; in fact, I have settled down nicely. Another tiff with the authorities to report, but nothing serious. You know how I hate getting up early, especially when it's pitch dark. Well, I had arranged with a confederate to sleep in late while he called my name on the roll-call. Very cunning: but I hadn't allowed for the contingency that the monumental fool might fail to wake up himself! Which was precisely what happened. I was lucky to get off with a reprimand.

My real objection, you know, is that there is so much time wasted with all this tomfoolery. I mean, if they wanted to check the roll-call why not do it at a decent hour? Doubtless I have mentioned this before, but when it comes to the invention of exhausting desultory pursuits, you can't beat the Army. Take yesterday: first, an inconsequent lecture; then an hour weathering the elements learning that fire hoses are used to put out fires with; finally I was detailed to sleep on a stretcher, equipped with a gas-mask, in a vacant shower room. The overall significance of these discomforts is — as you will have surmised, Courtney, a lemon!

Will continue later.

Pulled off another escapade yesterday. While officially I was watching for non-existent conflagrations, I was in fact twenty miles away bent on seeing the film, 'Bulldog Drummond Attacks'. But when I got there it was to find the cinema closed up: the show not being continuous!

Am extremely tired today, old lad; the Lewis frame is wilting. To begin with, some vandal ran off with the stretcher in the shower room which has been my bed for a week. All I could find were a couple of forms to sleep on, so I can tell you at first hand what it feels like to have a 'bed like a board'! Something to do with the latest influx of patients I presume, because I was woken from a fitful sleep at 5a.m. and spent the next four hours unloading another ambulance train. 200 German P.O.W.s this time. The stink on those wards is something grim.

To top it off, snow has been falling all night, and today Moston Hall — that exemplary exponent of prefab architecture, has been temporarily beautified. Many of the German prisoners have spicy names like, BOSSELMANN; BENDT; WINKLESHTINKER, and WIESSEN-SIFFTER.



Buzzed off to the family roost again yesterday for a bath and a palatable meal. It looks a picture in the snow, though the croquet lawn is somewhat blemished by the footprints of an inebriated blackbird. Fog curtailed the bus service, and not having a pass, I had to dodge the red-caps on the railway getting back. They must have been dozing as I was not challenged.

It may interest you to know that brother Peter is volunteering for the Navy this March, and nothing I can say will stop him. Boys will be boys! Even Meatball, I suppose, may be casting a longing eye at midget submarines.

Courtney old Rigor Mortis,

Feeling in the mood for gentle finger exercise, I have collared the Department typewriter and will endeavour to compose another of my fabulous rib-crackers, or should I say 'cervical snappers'?

Your letter of Dec. 5th reached me last Thursday, and although spangled by the usual gems of wit, definitely sounded a despondent note; a Brooklyn bridge-leaping attitude which must be countered at once. I am not censorious, old lad, for I too have groaned 'neath the yoke. I have never actually had to play basket-ball (a desultory pursuit), but I am sure that if I was ever put to the test, my efforts would be just as ludicrous as yours. At this juncture, I think I can claim to have mastered the wart-hog; but I admit there are discrepancies between the British and the American species. The British are uneducated and inclined to remain diffident towards an individual who wears an officer's beret, sleeps in silk pyjamas, and uses words like 'peripatetic', 'pusillanimous', and 'ratiocination' in every-day conversation. The American variety, as I know through past school experience, would not be put off my this sort of thing. They are born sadists and delight in boisterous practical jokes, such as putting lizards into the beds of more level-headed individuals. Americans — I maintain, Court-ney — just do not know how to take things easy. They eat too much vitamin-enriched bread.

You will, I am sure, be molested and cajoled from all sides. And there is only one thing to do. Think over your position, Courtney; think it over carefully. Is this course you are taking worth it? Wouldn't it be better to follow my illustrious example and chuck away the prospect of winning any sort of priviledge or position inside the system? Refuse to play ball and just gravitate till you find some forgotten corner — some niche where the duties are light, leaving time for more worthwhile pursuits such as another short-story? By the way, the Sponge King story is still in my father's hands whose watchword is Why Hurry?

This week-end, all being well, Wilbur and I will meet again to exchange news and views; he as my guest. A good time will indubitably be had by all. More about this later.

February 2nd 1945

Have been having more adventures: Graham — the roving medical orderly writes to you tonight. One of our many and varied duties is to escort convalescent soldiers home to their loved ones, and yesterday it was my unenviable task to accompany a T.B. case down to Paignton, Devon. I decided to return by a late train so that I could spend the night at home immersed in pale pink sheets, but of course the wretched puff-puff arrived late. So much so that I found myself alighting on Liverpool's rain-sodden platform at 12.30 a.m. There was no transport in operation, so I thumbed a ride through the Mersey Tunnel, and proceeded to walk the intervening seven miles home. The Wirral peninsular in the wee-small-hours is a desolate spot, and there was no chance of a lift. I tottered in at 3, but after a restorative rest I went to the local movie palace to see Rita Hayworth in 'Cover Girl'. I suppose she really does exist? I mean, those false eye-lashes, wigs, etc. suggest that the whole apparition might be a clever mock-up!

Wilbur came down on the 27th from Catterick on a forged pass, and stayed overnight. The next day (Sunday) we breakfasted on kidneys and bacon, and went for a brisk walk on the links clad in tweeds and swinging canes. Photos were taken, copies of which I will send anon. That eve we parted with a silent handshake.

February 6th 1945

Graham the Hardened Criminal is your correspondent

tonight. Have had yet another tiff with the authorities resulting in three days durance vile. A corporal whom I wouldn't buy a newspaper from were I wearing my tweed suiting hauled me over the coals for being hatless out of doors. Despite a brilliant defence, I failed to inveigle the desired acquittal. "Candidly, the whole incident strikes me as childish, sir," I said, "and hardly of paramount importance to the winning of the war."

Wilbur has also been in trouble: his forged passes failed to escape detection. While in jail he has started writing a short-story called 'Stalag Crashers'!

I hope you have not got a false impression of Moston, old lad. At times life is fraught with incident, but by-and-large it is a salubrious spot and even its faults are vastly outweighed by its proximity to the old homestead. But as the saying goes, 'what goes up must come down' (perhaps I mean 'all good things must come to an end'). Premonition of impending doom has come in the sudden posting to distant lands of a pal of mine, a sympathetic soul called Eddie, whose status in the organization is the same as my own. While such an expedition must tend to broaden the mind and enrich the soul under normal circs., I fear that under the Army's patronage the reverse effect must inevitably result!

*February 15th 1945*

Courtney old lad,

Both your birthday and Xmas remembrances have arrived and are gratefully accepted. Living up to my New Year Resolution, I have already perused the Edgar Wallace. Now, tell me, Courtney (for I am interested) what do you see in such prosaic stuff? This was a pot-boiler of the first order — a poor man's Sapper. I am not deprecating your generosity in sending me the gift, but am just giving you my frank opinion of the work. Turning to the second volume, I recall one of your favourite adages used to be, 'You cannot read a book by its cover.' I hope there is some truth in this, for on the back of this edition of Somerset Maugham's 'Strictly Personal' there is a photograph of the author, and a more nauseating specimen I cannot imagine! As this is his autobiography I fear I am in for an ordeal. From a cursory look at the contents it strikes me that he is one of those morbid souls devoid of humour. You wince at my narrow-mindedness, laddie, but I am becoming convinced that in a troubled world full of barbarism, hypocrisy, and too many wart-hogs, an essentially humorous philosophy is absolutely necessary. The trouble with this blighted world is that too many people take life too seriously. Look at the Germans, some of whom I have studied at close quarters; they are noted for their lack of humour. Could Hitler and his myrmidons have risen to power in any other nation?

The ridiculousness of the Nazis has been pursued and pinned by many cartoonists and satirists, but no one has done it with such devastating effect as Chaplin in 'The Great Dictator'. An immortal work for which he should be receiving unremitting adulation. Yet we see him hounded like P.G. Wodehouse; dragged before absurd courts of law on fatuous charges; compelled to submit to blood tests, etc. In my view, the man who created Adolf Hynkel and who conceived that little step-dance done with bread rolls impaled upon the ends of two table-forks (in 'The Gold Rush') should be allowed as many 'loose lilies' as he thinks he requires. The girls should be honoured to oblige.

Another anti-Nazi epic which needs no introduction is Leslie Howard's 'Pimpernell Smith' (called 'Mister V' in the U.S.) When Howard took a nose-dive into the Bay of Biscay the screen lost a great artist. The whole show was permeated with sound philosophy and characterization. I might add that the American version omitted a reference to P.G. in a telling scene aimed at denigrating the German sense of humour. The Reich Marshal is seen thumbing through a book by Wodehouse, and stops to read out a line to his aide: " 'The man in the beard smiled. Down in the forest something stirred.' Do you see anything funny there, Gottfried?" "No, Herr Reich Marshal. Nothing funny there," answers the side-kick. . . Hearty cachinnations from Graham in the back row!

Regarding our mutual enterprises: within the next ten days I will be dispatching a portfolio which I have been working on for weeks dealing exclusively with these things. This will include some astounding revelations concerning the technical side of our Art brought to my notice by a sympathetic major. Also some ideas for future stories with rough drawings of the characters. Last, but by no means least, the finished typescript of the Sponge King story will be included. Yes, Pop has produced the goods at last and it lies before me as I write in glorious resplendence — the impeccable work of a typing agency. Courtney, it is a masterpiece! I am myself surprised at its style and continuity: the words ooze across the page like honey. . . But enough of this eulogy: you yourself shall be the judge. One word of caution: please do not formulate plans for future work until you have received this all-important package, the contents of which, I might add, should dispel the deleterious effects of your present tribulations and should reveal the utterly meaningless nature of your current occupations.

P.S. I shall be sending two copies of the story: one to keep in a fire-proof safe, the other in your hat.


*March 18th 1945*

Courtney old lad,

You will have got my cable, so now just a note before I set foot into the Unknown. Your letter on pale pink paper popped in yesterday in time to catch me. Was grieved to find my suspicion substantiated; that my portrait photo never reached you. Never mind: I will do my best to procure another. I have before me a roll of snapshots taken some weeks ago showing myself and Wilbur in various moods.

These I will send. The indomitable Wilburforce has pulled another fast one! He has thrown up a comparatively tranquil sinecure as a clerk to accompany me overseas. As you will appreciate, his companionship on such a jaunt will be invaluable.

I will keep you well posted, old lad, but if letters are somewhat intermittent there is no cause for alarm. I have a feeling that this is to be the final mangle I shall have to negotiate, and it will doubtless cheer you to know that your old pal and colleague is in good spirits.

In your letter you scribble some nonsense about having to go into a bank. The thought appals me! The firm would have to close down. They could never meet the fees of the accountant who would have to clear up the mess. But seriously, I have no positive suggestion to make at this moment: I agree our work is still at the formative stage and it will be some time before we make any commercial headway. All I can say with certainty is that once we are out of this mess, the first move must be for you to visit England. Apart from anything else, we cannot stand on the same footing as writers until you know something of this country at first hand.

Was pleased with the press photo of P.G. but wonder if you discerned the underlying innuendos? Wodehouse is shown here wearing a black shirt (at least it looks black), his Prussian-style hair-cut clearly displayed, and talking to a woman with a German name! My congratulations go to the picture editor for some nifty work.

P.S. Have spent most of the evening on the telephone receiving fond farewells from the family. I had no idea the Lewis clan was so numerous.

*March 29th 1945*

Courtney old horse,

I am writing this missive on board ship, and Goodness

knows when it will be dispatched. As yet we have not set sail but are lying in dock at Liverpool o'ershadowed by the pretentious Liver Buildings. We have been here three days yet no attempt has been made to venture forth. Why the delay, I do not know. At a guess I would say the captain was in some doubt as to whether his vessel will float upon leaving its moorings; my own untutored view being that the matter is problematic. From one's earliest years one has a mental picture of a troop-ship as being somewhat over-crowded, but only those who have actually lived down among the cabbages and have slept two to the square yard can testify to the truth of this.

You will be pleased to hear that mutually sharing these unpromising quarters is the incorrigible Wilburforce. By informing the authorities that I am his cousin he has managed to squeeze himself onto the draft as a volunteer. I gather that his reason for doing so is an estrangement with his wife, and as I am the only chap he knows who repudiates womankind, he has joined me to forget his past and sally forth into the wilds of India to start a new life!

The grand assembly took place at the Depot, Aldershot, on the night of March 21st: a day of turmoil and utter confusion. Picture the scene: a vast shed like an aircraft hanger filled to bursting point with hundreds of men. It took hours to call the roll, and the only way I could ascertain whether Wilbur was with me or not was to wait with bated breath till I heard his name called. Interminably and at a snail's pace the doleful chant went on, until his place in the alphabet was reached and I stopped breathing altogether. The next second his name was called, and from somewhere far off I heard a voice answer, 'Here, sir.'

We were five days at Aldershot, and we spent most of the time enjoying ourselves one way or another — mostly at the Canadian Forces Club. We even tried a round of golf at Farnham, but failed to finish the course; a polite way of saying we hacked our way through an exhausting couple of holes! Hardly an exaggeration to say that by the end of our short stay at the barracks we had attracted the publicity to which we are accustomed. But we reasoned as follows: rather risk a few minor clashes with authority than submit docilely to the soul-destroying process in which we were engulfed.

Amidst all the frenzied activity of our departure I noticed a cat. It was sitting on the steps of one of the wooden buildings, dozing, and completely oblivious of the surrounding chaos. I've never seen the Sphinx, Courtney, but surely here is the answer to the proverbial riddle? Among a regiment of war-crazed wart-hogs in hobnail boots the cat alone was sane. And I said to myself: "Graham, old lad; copy that cat!"

At this point, a review of my present state of mind might be admissible. As you are well aware, I did not volunteer for this tea-party. But I was expecting it as it is the usual fate suffered by those who join the forces. The sword of Damocles was, in fact, late in falling, but when it eventually did fall, I was ready for it. I recall that I asked the gloating corporal who brought me the news if he knew the correct time.

I am sorry to be leaving England's salubrious shores, old lad; on the other hand, it strikes me that while I remain in this chain-gang, it does not really matter what country I am in. For the Army is ubiquitously the same, and like some chronic infestation, spoils anywhere it happens to be. If a company of soldiers moved into Buckingham Palace, the place would be like any other barracks in no time with a copy of Standing Orders nailed to the Throne Room door! Even during those few blissful respites when I was able to shake off the shackles, the thought that I would soon be returning was ever-present in my mind, overshadowing all I did like a heavy cloud.

*March 31st 1945*

We have just sailed! Passed out of the Mersey catching a brief glimpse of the Wirral. When this letter will reach you I am loathe to prognosticate as the voyage is said to last three weeks. However, I will keep adding to it until posting becomes possible.

I am writing this as I have half an hour to spare whilst

dodging P.T. Even on a troop-ship our time is regulated on the grounds that unless the men are given plenty to do, they get restless and cause trouble. So we have a varied programme of stimulating pursuits to follow; such as lifeboat drills, health inspections, mess duties, etc.

Now for a spot of local colour. The ship itself (the Strathmore) is a peacetime liner of prodigious tonnage. It was built by a band of workers under five feet high, and the entire structure seems to consist of a multitude of pipes with a liberal sprinkling of the usual nautical accoutrements — Blake screw slips, Robinson's disengaging gear, and the like. The decks have been divided into two sections. Section A, comprising about ten per cent of the total footage, is allocated to the two thousand odd troops, while Section B, being the other ninety per cent, is reserved exclusively for the officers. My living quarters, as previously stated, are situated in the bowels or duodenum of the vessel. One can sleep on the deck, in a hammock, or, as Wilbur and I prefer, in the empty hammock racks. And only the lucky bloke in the crow's nest has the priviledge of being alone.

April 1st 1945

Easter Morn — and what a morn! As I attempt to write these lines, the ship is doing its best to turn a somersault. Not only are tin hats, previously ensconced in the ceiling, dropping about like autumn leaves, but the entire regiment has succumbed to *mal de mer*. Everywhere I turn there is a puking wart-hog! The officers are not exempt either. They, however, do not puke on the spot but turn pale green, fumble for a pink pill, and murmur something about going to lie down!

Wilbur and I have so far weathered the storm, and taking full advantage of the situation, we consumed three Easter eggs each at breakfast plus several rashers of bacon. Then, after a somewhat unsteady saunter on deck during which we counted the numerous victims lying stretched out in rows, we refreshed ourselves with ginger beer and a tin of condensed milk!

April 10th 1945

As I write, we are steaming past the north coast of Africa. Dolphins are disporting themselves in the ship's wake, and all would be sublime if we were travelling under different auspices.

Out of the numberless thousands on board, only five have emerged with any pretensions to stage talent: two trombone players, an amateur conjuror, and myself and Wilburforce! Not a very strong company for a ship's concert party, to be sure, but good enough for an informal entertainment in one of the lounges. So far, Wilbur and I have performed our burlesque twice; not perhaps to resounding applause, but at least without having to dodge any rotten eggs. In the sketch (a product, of course, of the Lewis pen) Wilbur plays a colonel and I his aide (a monocled lieutenant: courtesy of Moston Hall Opthalmic Department). But I'm bound to admit, old lad, that the dialogue was somewhat lost on our untutored audience for whom the high-spot of the show was the moment when I pull a ladies stocking from my trouser pocket!

Referring to the aforementioned conjuror, a corporal in the Intelligence Corps; apart from being most proficient in the delicate art of prestidigitation, he is also a practising journalist and short-story writer. This latter attribute naturally interested me greatly, and I gave him our masterpiece for perusal. His opinion was disappointing; in fact, old lad, I am bound to tell you that he dismissed it as a non-starter from the commercial standpoint. He said he "wouldn't give it an inch of space."!He also asked me if we had written it for adults or children, which disconcerted me somewhat, I can tell you.

Of course I pointed out that it was our first effort, that

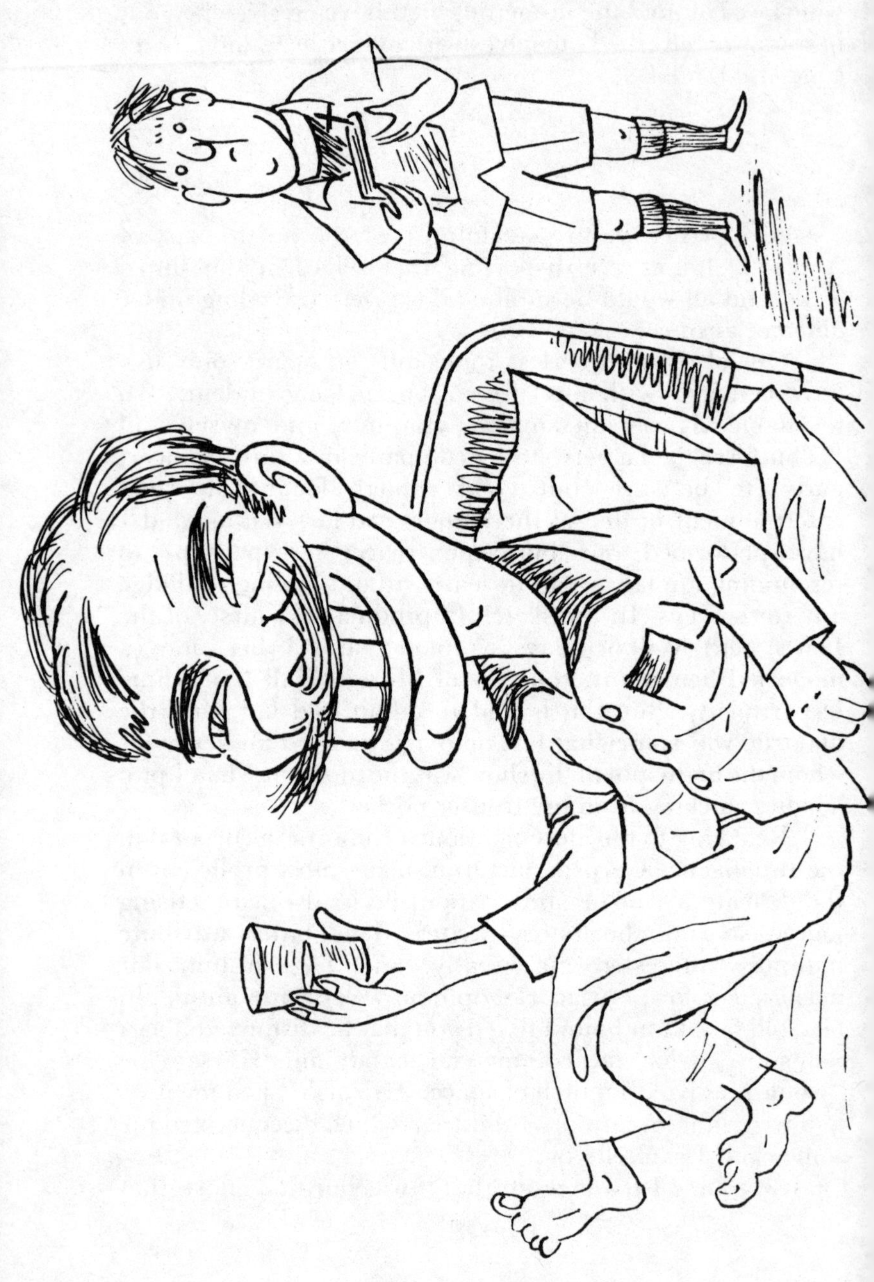

we wrote it by post on either side of the Atlantic Ocean. But thinking it over, old lad, I am inclined to acquiesce with his views — those of an experienced writer. The story is a masterpiece, but not — I am loathe to admit — perfect. Our style needs work on it — years of assiduous toil. We have achieved something but not enough to think of publication. He was most encouraging about my cartoons, on the other hand, and I drew his caricature.

To digress: although I forgot to bring your Maugham with me, I procured one of his novels from the ship's 'library'. But as it was devoid of both cover and title page, I cannot tell you its name. The word 'Maugham' was only just discernible. I acknowledge your impeccable taste, Courtney; he is the goods. There is an underlying contempt towards mankind which is most appealing. Poor sense of humour, though.

One of his observations deprecated the human race for being obsessed with insignificant trifles, a point which is admirably applicable to the armed forces. Both Wilbur and myself continue to be plagued by this demented obsession, and the other day found us both on a charge for some paltry misdemeanour (avoiding P.T. to be exact). I got five days c.b. (I suppose in present circumstances this means 'confined to boat'?) and Wilbur, seven. I completed my sentence, but Wilbur — very judiciously — collapsed in the middle of his with sun-stroke! He was scrubbing decks at the time. I found him later in the ship's infirmary where I hastened bearing gifts. He was happily ingurgitating limejuice, and seemed his usual irrepressible self. But he had been unconscious for five hours, and I understand that doctors, priests, and other functionaries had been standing by expecting a burial at sea! They don't know Wilbur. You will be pleased to hear that he is once more back in circulation and seemingly none the worse for his experience.

(Later)

Just docked at Port Said. The heat in our little hold is intolerable and as I write, I pause occasionally to wipe a be-dewed brow. The town's architecture might have been designed by Billy Butlin of Skegness fame. Strange crafts litter the harbour, and their owners are eager to dance the Egyptian rhumba if showered with cigarettes from our decks.

So now it's on through the Suez Canal and down the Red Sea. In ten days time we should reach Bombay.

P.S. I have been taking the liberty of pinning up some cartoons on the ship's notice board. My latest, showing a sea of hammocks on the mess deck, got a jubilant reception.


*May 6th 1945*

Courtney old lad,

The last letter I wrote you was rather a lengthy chronicle composed on the boat, and which might take anything up to six months to reach you. Exactly how these letters go, I don't know. They may wing their way via Tasmania or perhaps skip across through Tibet. Whichever route they take, it strikes me that a long time must elapse before delivery. So what I'm going to do is this. I shall send this letter home by Air Mail, which takes under a week, then Mother can forward it on to you. I deem it judicious for you to adopt the same method.

To proceed. Life has been replete with events lately. We reached Bombay on the 21st, and after the usual maelstrom, tottered onto the quay in the small hours. We were then herded into cattle trucks which were crawling with ants, and transported along the Jabalpur line to Deolali, which translated into English must mean, 'the last word in desolation'.

The first shock came the following morning when a cursory scrutiny of the camp notice-board informed me that the authorities had placed myself and Wilbur on different draft lists. I was so incensed at this that I went straight along to the Camp H.Q. and demanded to see the Commandant.

He turned out to be a major of sympathetic aspect, and —
laddie, you could have knocked me out with a baseball bat!
When I made my protest, he expunged both our names from
the lists and retained us for work at the Depot. There was one
condition: I had to promise to paint him some murals at the
new camp up the road. Well, I've never thought of myself as
a budding Michelangelo, but with the alternative a
lingering death in a Burmese swamp, it did not take me
longer than two seconds to accept the offer.

And that's the current position. Wilbur is going in for
secretarial work, while I am now on the staff of the
Education Department. I have heard nothing further about
wall pictures: my duties oblige me to do anything from
designing a poster explaining the deadly habits of the Deolali
mosquito to drawing a blueprint of the Four Foot Field
Latrine.

We have left our tents, and the camp has moved up the
road to avoid the worst effects of the impending monsoon.
My new quarters are airy and comfortable; a fact which has
not escaped the local scorpions which also abide there!

As you are no doubt waiting for impressions of India,
that Star of the East, to flow from the Lewis pen, a few words
of local colour may not be out of place at this juncture. Apart
from scorpions and mosquitoes that make a noise like a
steam whistle as they approach, rumour has it that king
cobras form part of the scenery though as yet I have not seen
one. Add to this a motley assortment of pestilential diseases
(including the bubonic plague) and a scorching sun, and you
have a thumb-nail sketch of my present salubrious habitat.

The terrain itself is decidedly moth-eaten, and as there
is so much of it there are nothing like enough trees to go
round. The actual denizens of this blighted spot are utterly
impoverished and breed prolifically. They appear to subsist
mainly on the remnants of our never delectable meals. They
carry piles of household utensils on their heads, large
numbers of insects on their bodies, and do not seem to wear
any clothes until the age of sixteen when they start with a fig
leaf or its local equivalent.

Speaking of our delectable meals; despite the fact that we are in the tropics where fresh fruits and vegetables abound, with characteristic obtuseness the authorities persist in feeding us traditional Army grub such as beef stew, boiled potatoes, and cocoa. Inedible swill, old lad; and save for the numerous 'wallahs' who tramp around with a grocer's shop on their heads, I should assuredly expire through malnutrition.

Well, Courtney — must terminate. As I write, all the Nazi war criminals are committing suicide, so perhaps our days under the yoke are numbered.

*May 21st 1945*

Courtney old lad,

Try writing to me here at the Depot as an experiment. Post it Air Mail and we'll see how long it takes to reach me. The one I've just received dated April 24th took four weeks. Admittedly it was forwarded by my companionable brother who may have kept it in his pocket a week or two along with his bits of string, catapults, etc. Incidentally, in August he too becomes a victim to that bird of prey — the Army. A few details about the behaviour of this bird might amuse you. It beats its wings with regulation strokes of thirty inches, but can only get into the air when there is a large brass band playing 'Colonel Bogey'. It has a red, white, and blue crest on its head which it raises at sunrise and lowers at sunset when it goes to roost. . . You may enlarge this picture in your spare time, old lad; however, for the nonce let us drop the subject.

Once again your letter evinces a distinct yearning for Brooklyn Bridge. Pull yourself together, Courtney! This is only a transient phase. Such impressions of Emory that have filtered through to me suggest that it is not the ideal venue for a struggle with one's soul, and you have my sympathy. It may console you to know that both Wilbur and Desmond, to a lesser degree, are in the same straits. Desmond once showed me a notebook in which he had inscribed various impressions and opinions, an attempt to crystallize his views; while Wilbur, under my influence I admit, has come to realize that his imperturbable aplomb is but a shallow mask. At present he has no idea where he is or where he's going. His vocation remains shrouded in mystery. Of one thing only he is certain: whatever it is, he is going to be the top of it!

Turning to more mundane topics: since I last wrote the war in Europe has ended. A historic day and a milestone on the highway that leads to the crossroads where we shall meet again. I expect you heard Churchill's peroration announcing Germany's defeat? He finished with the words, "Love God; Honour the King; Brittania Rules The Waves!" which in my view wins the Golden Corn Cob for Puffed Up Oratory.*

Of course a Camp shindy or Victory Celebration was at once declared, which afforded possibilities for diverse entertainment in my and Wilbur's estimation. That evening we resuscitated our cabaret sketch (the one we performed on board ship), but for the last time, old lad, the very last time! Mind you, we could hardly have foreseen that our corpulent Adjutant, bottled to the eyebrows, would stagger onto the stage in the middle just before the big moment when I pull out the silk stocking, bellowing, "You're hopelesh! You're hopelesh!" But that's what he did, old lad; and it would have taken a seasoned pro to carry on under the circumstances.

Anyway, the next day we were presented with a golden opportunity for taking revenge. A fancy-dress football match was the order of the day, so Wilbur dressed up as the Adjutant and came onto the field brandishing a beer bottle. I followed behind him holding up a large poster on which were daubed the words, 'Drink More Bass'. The joke went down well!

*What Churchill actually said was: "Advance Brittania — Long live the cause of Freedom — God save the King."

I am still on the Depot staff here, but my position is precarious. The Major, I have discovered, is a man who, in order to alleviate the tedium of barracks life, collects protegés. I am one of them, and currently my task, believe it or not, is to complete a series of caricatures of staff personnel. When I have done so I shall be tossed aside like a spent match! Describe my position as that of a slot machine running out of bars of chocolate, Courtney, and you have it.

My caricature of the Major himself made him look like Mickey Mouse, and I confess that it was with some trepidation that I showed him the finished work of art. I needn't have worried. I won't say he laughed exactly, but he sort of purred — like a cat licking a saucer of milk. The latest news is that I have been requested to produce a cartoon for a local Army newspaper.

By and large, you know, this present sojourn constitutes the most salubrious of my career. Deolali is indubitably a blighted spot, but what more could I ask than being paid my pound a week, or its rupee equivalent, for producing drawings and caricatures? I share a spacious office with a congenial companion, and am untrammelled by routine camp discipline. Last but not least, there is Wilbur who, I must tell you, has netted himself a sinecure almost as felicitous as my own.

When he was a lad (he is now twenty-three, you know) he was down at Oxford and used to dabble in psychology, logic, hypnotism and that sort of thing. With this basis plus the Wilburforce personality and drive he has landed the job of psychiatrist's aide down at the B.M.H. with the long-term prospect of becoming a fully-fledged psychiatrist with the Umbrella Men (the Airborne Division). I saunter into his office to find him busy at work assisting in the endless task of diagnosing the mental derangements among N.C.O.s! No wonder he has so little spare time. . . His boss is a colonel named Branksome whom Wilbur calls 'Branky'.

His latest case concerns a Private named _______ (confidential) described as the sixteenth of seventeen children! His peculiarity is a penchant for stabbing people in the behind with a bush knife, and when questioned as to his motive in perpetrating these assaults, he is alleged to have replied: "If you had been obliged to wear the cast-off clothing of fifteen brothers all your life, you'd do it too." A perplexing case, Courtney, and one which will tax Branky's powers to the utmost.

Write me more often, old lad.

Toodle-oo, and as Churchill said when the Germans surrendered — God Save the King and Rule Brittania!

P.S. Have been seeing an awful lot of movies lately. But none of them worth mentioning, except perhaps the latest Laurel and Hardy, and even this one wasn't too good. They are still past-masters of slapstick comedy but sadly in need of a script-writer who can fully display their talents. Laurel rendering 'Mares-eat-oats' on the concertina was the highlight of this production.

June 10th 1945

Courtney old lad,

Nothing more from you since my last; but I received a letter from Desmond the other day. You remember I had deemed him to have sunk without trace in the Ballykinlar bogs? Well, if the letter had been posted in far off Kuala Lumpur or somewhere it would not have surprised me, but — believe it or not — it came from somewhere in India! By means of a Cinderella-like transformation, the old boy is now a Sergeant Glider Pilot attached to the R.A.F. Now all we need is for you to come along and the four of us can throw a party and see the Taj Mahal together!

By the way, has that portrait photo of me reached you yet? (The one I had taken at Aldershot.) I sent a print to Desmond at the time, and now he has confided that he thinks it, "supercilious, cynical, proud and bored; handsome and soft-skinned." Not bad, what!

My position as Camp Jester and Mad Artist continues

— I am happy to report. But since I last wrote, a certain friction has been developing between me and the disciplinarians (predictable, I suppose). I think I mentioned that being on the staff I escaped the usual bull and what-not. True enough, but this does not mean that I had escaped the eagle eye of the C.S.M. — a hardbitten regular of the old school. The day came when I received a direct order from him (sent by special messenger!) craving my presence on parade the next morning. Thanks to Tootles, the barrack-room valet, my attire on this occasion was immaculate, and when the big moment arrived I was able to face the inspection with confidence. "Ha!" cried the sergeant-major after an intense scrutiny. "Less of the artist and more of the soldier, I hope." Which gave me a big laugh!

But I could see he was out to grind me 'neath his iron heel, and was just waiting for the right opportunity.

This came the following Saturday; in fact, I presented it to him on a plate. There was one of these super-parades. I remember imparting my misgivings to Wilbur the day before, and he laughed and said he would see me in ten days time when I had completed my sentence. Well, the day duly dawned and Tootles, as usual, did his stuff. My attire was impeccable from the tip of my cap badge down to the gleaming studs on the soles of my shining boots. There was just one thing wrong: out of the four hundred soldiers on parade, I was the only one wearing long trousers! Of course it was too late to change, and I just stood there sweating — hoping the C.S.M. wouldn't notice!

The next morning I duly faced the charge, and it was some comic opera, I can tell you. to accede to some absurd formality I was stripped of my web belt with the result that my loose-fitting trousers instantly fell to my knees. I stood stiffly to attention, Courtney, inwardly shaking with mirth, while the C.S.M. and his henchmen rushed frantically in all directions looking for a safety pin! You won't believe this, old horse, but it's true.

Eventually they found one and I was marched before the judge — a captain. I reeled off my defence: namely that I

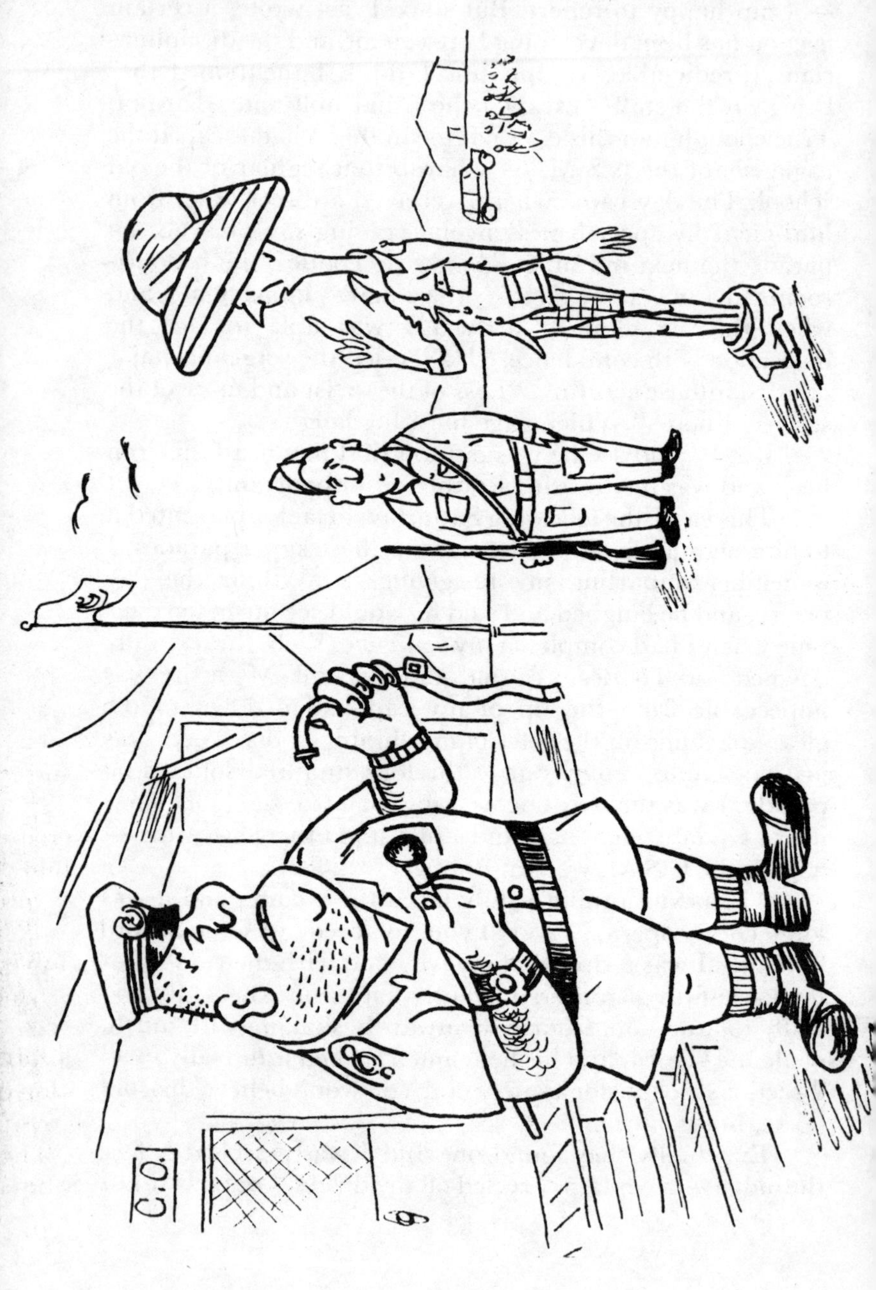

had spilt red paint onto my shorts while working on a poster, and had been unable to get them washed in time. I did not anticipate for a moment that he would swallow this threadbare stuff, and braced myself for the sentence. But he did, Courtney! And I left his kindly presence without a stain on my character (or my shorts, for that matter!).

A hilarious proceeding as I'm sure you will concur. But I did not get off scot-free. The lion in the form of the C.S.M. may have been deprived of his prey, but he was not going to let it get away without a scratch. He had me marched under escort to the regimental barber where my by no means luxurious head of hair was sheared brutally from my scalp. A sad event, Courtney; for how can an artist commune with his Muse when devoid of natural foliage? I know I have your sympathy.

That's not the end of the story either. Wilbur and I must have been born under the same sign or something, because I'm dashed if he wasn't placed on two charges the next day. Although he managed to wangle his way out of the first, there was nothing he could do about the second which netted him seven days. A sorry plight, you might think, yet Wilbur took it lightly. Despite the fact that he was officially confined to barracks, we went to the movies that evening. The plan was that we should meet in the picture house, so I sat near the door and gave him the pre-arranged signal, a hacking cough, when I saw him come in. Worked beautifully, though I almost failed to recognize the old boy as he was wearing a pair of dark glasses and a heavy muffler; rather a conspicuous disguise, I thought, considering the climate and the fact that it was dark outside. Anyway, there were no police about and all went according to Cocker!

*June 20th 1945*

These are great days, old lad, great days! True, the char wallah has just expired suddenly — one suspects poisoned by his own tea. They keep it simmering all day on a charcoal burner, and it's a wicked brew. But the tragedy, sad as it is, pales into insignificance alongside the joyous fact that Desmond and I have met once more.

It happened last Sunday afternoon. I was in my sanctuary working on a map of the camp when a corporal with a monstrosity of a moustache sauntered in and said: "Don't I strike a chord?" For a second I looked at him stupidly; then recognition dawned and the next moment I was shaking hands with my old pal. The bottom having fallen out of his gliding (not his glider!) he had been sent to Deolali of all places for recategorization. Truly a providential posting.

We picked up Wilbur, and the three of us had a roaring evening dining at the Kwang Tung Chinese Restaurant, and making all the chinks jump by ordering lobster fu-yong in cream jugs! Later, we all had a hearty laugh watching the film, 'Since You Went Away' — the ultimate in corny war propaganda. For the last three evenings there has been no let-up in our celebrations, made possible on the strength of Desmond's sergeant's pay; and the three of us send you our salutations and regrets that you were unable to be with us, as I am sure you would have wished to be.

I have become convinced, old lad, that when this mad interlude is finally over we must all join forces. Last night I put forward a tentative suggestion — a suggestion for forming a club consisting of the four of us; a club which I thought might be named the Square Peg Club. Both Wilbur and Desmond applauded the idea, so let me know what you think. Of course, it is merely a nebulous notion at present; but given time and thought, the aspirations and function of this egregious circle would begin to take shape. Desmond proposed that you join us for a caravan tour of battle-torn Europe as soon as we have won our releases from the binding chains and weighty balls. Wilbur agreed, but when he suggested bringing Beryl Cynthia (his dream girl) along, Desmond and I poured water down his neck until he promised to reconsider the idea.

Of course, the dominant topic of conversation was Desmond's immediate future; and it was duly decided that an attempt should be made to wangle a transfer into the medical corps. Wilbur's inside knowledge of mental crack-ups was a big help here, and he suggested a persecution mania with hysterical symptoms as the type of disorder to aim at. He evolved a plan whereby Desmond would report sick the next morning and complain in broken tones to the M.O. that his bed, belongings, and clothing were overrun by red ants; that his food was crawling with ants, etc. etc. A marvellous scheme, old lad, which Wilbur swore would get him straight into the psychiatric wing at the hospital where he (Wilbur) would be able to control the situation.

Looking back on it, I can see that the scheme was doomed from the start as there is no one less hysterical by temperament than Desmond, or less likely to imagine himself crawling with red ants. Full of resolve, he reported sick as planned, but when his turn came the congenital idiot lost his nerve and complained of bunions! Ah, well, Courtney, we did our best. So if they send him to the Burmese swamps he has only himself to blame.


June 21st 1945

Bombshell! Life for me seems to be a never-ending series of shocks. What's more, I can't stand much more of it. I must find a niche somewhere. I am being posted *tomorrow*. Having tired of my presence, the Depot Dictators are dispatching me to somewhere on the Northwest Frontier near the Khyber Pass where the chances are you will be knifed by a maurauding tribeman. I have tried to see the Major but he is elsewhere.

We are all in the depths of despondency.

More later but must post this now.


57

June 25th 1945

Courtney old lad,

I am writing this bulletin from the Sandes Soldier's Home, Rawalpindi, during a much-needed break in my journey which takes six days. The sequestered atmosphere of the place, which has *real beds* — not charpoys, is conducive to repose and meditation.

You would think that the British Raj, having occupied India for so long, would have supplied the railways with steam engines that were a little more advanced in design than Stephenson's Rocket. This, however, is not the case. The machine which dragged me up here from Deolali, in what I would describe as a lurching cattle truck, wheezed and snorted like a chronic asthmatic in the last stages of the disease. God knows what tomorrow will bring, but if it's anything like the last three days and two nights I'll blow a gasket. It's insufferably hot, and I have been sedulously drained of my meagre resources by predatory natives on station platforms.

I am travelling with one other man — our destination, Razmak; the last outpost in the wilds of Afghanistan 7000 feet above sea level in the heart of the Himalayas. I must have been born under an itinerant star, or something, Courtney. I mean, the last outpost — dash it! The *very* last!

There was nothing I could do to get out of this, though the three of us (Wilbur, Desmond, and I) must have thought of every permutation before giving it up as hopeless. I caught my last glimpse of them sauntering disconsolately into the twilight as my train pulled out last Saturday, and God knows when I shall see them again. . .

Time for sleep, old lad. I am very tired.


June 27th 1945

I pen these lines — somewhat shakily — in a transit

camp at a hell-hole called Bannu. Mercifully we have been granted a thirty-six hour respite to await the next convoy, otherwise I must assuredly have expired. The heat is the worst I have ever known. It is impossible to sleep, and the metal bedstead, even at night, is too hot to touch. My comb has melted!

Yesterday we crossed the notorious Sind Desert on a small gauge railway like a toy train. Before we started they loaded a huge block of ice into every compartment, and we just sat and watched it melt while we sweated like pigs! Physically, Graham Lewis is now a broken reed: besides exhaustion, I am suffering from constipation, and — though you won't believe it — a chill!

Even the toy train ends at Bannu, and the last lap of this dreadful journey is traversed by a convoy of armed lorries. We start at dawn!

*June 28th 1945*

Reached the fort safely. A hair-raising ride. Imagine a winding trail up into the mountains; a wild and desolate landscape; hair-pin bends with a sheer drop thousands of feet into the valleys below. The lorries were driven by special Indian drivers with others armed with rifles aboard as a precaution against possible ambush by bands of Afghan brigands called Pathans.

Ramzak itself is a walled compound and is heavily guarded: no one is allowed outside the gates. At first glance, it looks like the goods. Staff living quarters at the hospital are very comfortable; it is gloriously cool, and there is an English-style park with green grass and a herbaceous border. Last but not least, there are no women. No women at all, old lad! They have never penetrated as far as this Himalayan fastness.

Will write further details anon, but as I say, my first impression is very favourable. I believe I have found my niche at last!

Courtney old lad,

This is just a covering note to accompany the enclosed literature.

Life here is proceeding according to Cocker. I am on the surgical ward — the slave of the bed-pan and penicillin squeezer. Currently my patients include a Gurkha with a gastric ulcer who has a tube sticking out of his belly, and a brigand eviscerated in a brawl. Both patients and their attendants are men of very few words. The two young surgeons look upon the place as a private art gallery, and consider the compound humerus fracture to be their outstanding exhibit.

Turning to the enclosed: the short novel by Maugham, 'Up At The Villa', is a masterly study of the Empire-builder which shows clearly the shortcomings of this species in the evolutionary scheme of things. If you haven't already read it, old lad, you are in for a treat. As for the magazine, 'Victory': the name will warn you to approach it with caution, it's an all-India Army publication. However, the full-page cartoon on page 9 does something to redeem this particular number. Perhaps not my best effort, old lad, and the reproduction is poor; but a step in the right direction! As a matter of fact, I had no idea they were going to use it until I saw it in the mag a few days ago. I think the editor may have been captivated by the little Japanese general with the big sword, third from the right!

Incidentally, have you noticed the appearance of certain photographs in current periodicals depicting defeated German generals hobnobbing with their Allied oppos over glasses of champagne and what-not? Despite the Monty-Rommel cameraderie, nobody seems to understand that war is a game of chess to these men. Each respects the other as do opponents in a chess match; and when it is all over there is nothing for them to do except analyse each other's battle tactics or play each other at chess, perhaps!

In closing, I cannot refrain from observing that today is

Inebriate's Day in the U.S. A truly auspicious date celebrating, as it does, one of the far too few occasions in history when the British empire-builder was given a swift kick in the seat of his pants and thrown out on his ear!

July 25th 1945

Courtney old lad,

With startling celerity another month has almost sped by, and as the sun wanes in the West we see that eminent savant, Professor Lewis, closeted in his mountain laboratory peering earnestly down the microscope. The evening breeze is cool, and a Himalayan mango sways slightly 'neath the open window. What superficial observer could tell that history was in the making? Passing a well-bromo-cresol-stained hand across his furrowed brow the scientist submits his instrument to one last peer before pushing it gently away with a muttered 'Eureka!' just as his faithful Sepoy appears bearing a pot of black coffee. The elusive malaria germ has been traced and isolated. . .

Here, in a nutshell, Courtney, you have my activities for the past three weeks, and I trust for many weeks to come. Razmak is the gem I thought it was. I have found my niche! I have been taken off ward duty and appointed to the Clinical Side Room, a two-man laboratory. Our main function is the examination of blood-slides, sputum and things with a view to medical diagnosis. There is, however, quite a lot of spare time on this job, and I am carrying on a spot of private research which may — or may not — ultimately appear in the pages of the British Medical Journal. I have discovered that two drops of Xylol Pure administered every two hours to a bowl of white carnations turns them blue and they die! A pointless discovery you may say, old lad; yet it is quite possible that Alexander Flemming noticed far less striking results during the initial stages before he discovered penicillin.

61

The name of my faithful Sepoy, by the way, is Ellan Din, and I cannot praise him too highly. True, we speak different languages and our conversation is somewhat laconic in consequence, but there is a mutual understanding between us that does not need to be expressed in words. This bond has lately been strengthened by the multitude of petty crimes that we have had to cover up. For example: it was he who supported my claim to innocence when I broke the bottle of Carbol Fuschin; and it was I who saved him from a miserable fate when he failed to show up last Sunday. Truly a staunch friend, Courtney, and I might add — the possessor of a sense of humour.

The latest news from Wilbur is that he is working at Poona. You have heard of Poona — the fabulous citadel of empire-builders? Desmond is still doing nothing at Deolali. Both send their regards to you. Wilbur added: "Courtney is indubitably in a worse position than any of us." He's right. I have not had a letter from you since I arrived here but I suppose things with you are pretty much the same? Whatever my own trials and tribulations, I have always been vaguely aware that I was slowly gravitating towards my rightful niche in the system. But there can be 'no change' in your case. In addition, you are without confidants, and have been for two years now.

Entertainment here is rather scarce, but there are books to be found and a cinema in the compound. The other night I saw the Somerset Maugham movie, 'Christmas Holiday'. 'Good entertainment' sums it up I suppose, though to have been properly cynical in the true Maugham manner they should have shot Deanna Durbin at the end. Her almost inaudible last words, "So this is love" were pure Hollywood corn.

Then there was the Ensa Concert; a rare event. The entire staff attended — except myself, and incredulity and consternation at my 'perverse' refusal to join them was widely voiced. I remained adamant and did not go for obvious reasons. I mean, old lad, would you enjoy sitting in the middle of a thousand wart-hogs guffawing at a dreary string of bluish jokes and gazing goggle-eyed at an ensemble of pink legs? They may be able to press-gang you into the forces, but they can't compel you to see their _______ entertainment!

July 28th 1945

As you can see I had a little trouble with my pen today while changing the ink. There is quite an assortment of potions in the lab, so I decided to try toning the usual purple down a bit. The new iridescent shade is the result of mixing Benedicts Solution with sulphuric acid and adding a pinch of magnesium sulphate. Unfortunately the pen itself has turned partially green and shows signs of melting, while the ink is inclined to fade. I have visions of you staring bewilderedly at half a dozen blank sheets of paper! Think I'll address the envelope in pencil, just in case.

I have just made the ghastly discovery, old horse, that I am rapidly going bald! I wake up at nights in a cold sweat with visions of billiard balls and hard-boiled eggs! Your phrase, "a sheep without its wool, a bird without its feathers. . ." is indelibly etched on my mind. My Indian barber informs me that it is to do with the hot weather, and I have purchased a magic potion which is guaranteed infallible. There are no visible waste lands yet, but I count my hairs every night! Certainly the ones that are falling out look a lot stronger since I started using the stuff.

You know what a disgruntled creature the wart-hog is when deprived of women and unlimited beer? Conversation in the barrack room has been somewhat acrimonious of late. Of course, I keep well out of it. I've been here a month now during which time they have been inspecting me tentatively — like a cat does a ball of wool. They have come to the conclusion I won't bite, but that's as far as they've got! Of course, you know I adopt a sort of idiot Algy Longworth pose so as to keep them at arm's length. There's no alternative really, as trying to discuss anything abstract with them at all, besides being a complete waste of time, is utterly enervating. The wart-hog's concentration is limited; his mind constantly wanders from the point, and when out of his depth he either becomes obnoxious and begins to swear or else he takes his stand on some dogma or other which he repeats till he is blue in the face. In effect, he has closed the discussion.

I made the mistake today of getting involved in one of these fruitless arguments. My opponent, who would make a first-class beer barrel washer or pit pony boy (I met a couple of these at Deolali and I know the symptoms), obstinately refused to reconsider his claim that he is the mental equal of Bernard Shaw. Of course, he has never heard of Shaw, but as it is his contention that he is the mental equal of any living man, it follows that the Sage of Ayot must be included. I agree heartily with Shaw's remark that democracy (meaning government by the people) must prove disastrous in the end. *For* the people, yes; but not *by* the people. And I am talking about parliamentary government not 'mob rule'. It was Shaw, you know, who quipped, "The more I see of men, the more I like dogs" which I am seriously thinking of having embroidered in coloured wool and hanging up in a frame over my bed!

The main part of the argument was, as usual, about the war, during which I ventilated my views that the whole thing was a ghastly mistake from start to finish. He agreed that my pacifism was morally laudible but attacked it for being unworkable: 'the philosophy of defeat' he called it. When I pointed out that only those who believed in fighting used terms like 'victory' or 'defeat' he was completely nonplussed!

Boiling it all down, I think what he found incomprehensible was my complete detachment from the entire proceedings; and of course, like you, I view the world through the eyes of a detached observer. (This is the reason why it all seems so ridiculous.) When I am on an inspection parade or forced onto the back of a lorry complete with kit-bag, etc., I feel myself — not as one of the rest of them, but as a sort of disembodied onlooker. This attitude is maintained because I have no sympathy whatever with anything going on. Conversely, when I am hobnobbing with one of the Square Pegs I do not feel this detachment to anything like the same extent. This is not because I have ceased to be 'out of it' but because I feel myself to be in the company of someone who is 'out of it' also. . .

This effusive passage of purple philosophy has probably knocked you endways, old lad! My apologies: it must be something to do with the Himalayan ozone!


August 18th 1945

Dear Courtney,

Meandered nonchalantly into our sitting room this morning to be struck between the eyes by a hideous lithograph impinged on the wall: further scrutiny revealing that it was supposed to be something by Paul Nash entitled The Vernal Equinox. If this is an example of the Art Education for the Forces scheme I am dead against it. There are enough eyesores in an Army barracks without employing Paul Nash to supply more.

The scene from this window as the sun dips low over the massive mountain ranges would make Paul Nash chuck away his paints and take up stamp collecting, always assuming he is not colour blind. I mention it, old lad, because it marks the end of the second year since our parting. And what a year! No one can deny that it has been a year among years. Heading the list of momentous happenings is indubitably the catastrophic detonation of the atomic bomb. A close second, the end of the war in both theatres adumbrating, as it does, the roseate prospect of our eventual release from 'durance vile'. At last, laddie, it is possible to envisage a future without a protracted sojourn in a padded or possibly zinc-lined cell as the culminating misery! The stage has now been cleared and will shortly be set for a new act, which may well be the finale. I am again thinking of the Bomb, which threatens to destroy the entire playhouse.

65

Philosophers the world over must be shaking their heads in despair at this revelation that human vanity is so colossal, so insane that it has dared to experiment with the power of the sun. The sun: the centre of our universe and the source of our existence! All scientists, apart from those who invent albumenized baby foods and the like, ought to be locked away with the other dangerous lunatics, in my opinion. To say that they don't know what they are doing is only half the truth: they don't know and they don't care! Looking back through history, it is hard to avoid coming to the sombre conclusion that there is a fundamental desire for self-destruction implanted in the human race.

Of course, none of these misgivings have clouded the minds of my fellow workers to whom the end of the Japanese war was greeted with much merry-making. Last Thursday having been declared another Gala Day with copious supplies of free beer laid on, it was the early hours of the morning before the wart-hog finally collapsed on his bed having been sick all over the floor! A colourful evening, due to the effects of alcohol being so varied. Some get violent and fling bottles about; others merely become horribly ill. Some sink into a semi-coma, while the luckiest become increasingly jubilant. The next morning, however, they all feel the same!

To change the subject, Courtney, I know you would like to hear the latest news concerning the other two members of our band? In Desmond's case, there isn't any: characteristically he has vanished into the void in search of further adventure. Wilbur's last dispatch was rather sensational. It included a photograph of him standing on his head sucking a mango, and announced that he was awaiting repatriation to England pending a discharge from the Army on psychiatric grounds! I can't elaborate on this further, old lad. The best I can do is quote Wilbur's own comment: "Patience, laddie; explanation later." If I don't sound surprised it's because I know to expect the unexpected from this irrepressible being. He is capable of anything.

As for myself, I fear my days as a microbe-watcher may

be numbered. I sauntered in to work the other morning languidly sniffing a crysanthamum which I intended to make magenta, to find half the staff had disappeared. Unprecedented. What was I to do? In effect, there I was in charge of the District Laboratory! Well, as you know, Graham Lewis never admits defeat, so I waded into the work which I completed with what I imagined to be consummate skill. Doubts began to creep into my mind, however, when I began to receive threatening notes from doctors all over the hospital. Finally, one of these — an Indian officer — appeared in person wildly brandishing my report and swearing loudly in Punjabi or some such tongue. All very disquieting after my hours of toil. I was almost cross-eyed with staring down the _______ tube. But you know, old lad, I'm bound to admit that one microbe looks much like another to me. They're all very pretty things: some of them have got pink spots.

(Later)

Stop Press! My friend the Clerk has just appeared waving a much-effaced and dog-eared envelope: your first letter since May 21st. Will comment after perusal. . .

My dear old lad, you fail to comprehend the importance of your missives, even though most of them ought to bear the usual signatures which witnesses customarily append to Last Wills and Testaments. Picture to yourself a lonely Graham perched on a lofty summit; his only consolation being good books (which he hasn't got) and inspiring letters (which he hasn't got). His mother has posted a parcel of books which he expects to reach him sometime before next Whitsuntide, while as for letters. . .The lamentable absence of any from 'the band' is only emphasized by the effusions he has been receiving from his loyal Aunti; the latest devoted to describing the summer garden party! She has sent me a large photo of a wart-hog — the animal variety, cut from a magazine. A ferocious looking beast with a tusk: apparently it eats its young.

I will refrain from censure, old horse, but when you say

you spent most of your leave pickling your brains in your seven weighty volumes on Robert E. Lee, I think I am entitled to make a mild protest! You see, my first ecstatic impressions of Razmak (mainly due to the mountain air, I think) have long since worn off, being replaced by a growing depression. Without the presence of any confidant or letters from 'the band' I am a prey to the inimical effects of solitude and 'barrack-roomitis'. So do write me more often, Courtney.

Now, you mention your youth. On page 3 you remark that it has been an unhappy one. This I can well believe: it must have been a running battle against the conventions of Lynchburg life with no solace except my belated own. In contrast, my own youth has been tempestuous but extremely interesting and educating despite the moments of despair when my surroundings close in on me, so to speak.

There must be something about me which instinctively attracts misfits, though sometimes they don't know they are misfits until they have met me! When I met Wilbur down at Aldershot almost a year ago, he was an ex-commando devoted to his wife and child. The model e.b. in fact, except for his flamboyance. Yet I noticed some intangible quality (call it 'individualism' if you like) which developed with our friendship, eventually inspiring him to desert his wife (she had been consorting with one of your countrymen which afforded an excuse), and volunteer for India — an emancipated soul!

So far as I can see, the only remedy for your present plight is to emulate Wilbur and get out of it as quickly as possible, and I confidently await the obligatory photograph showing you standing on your head masticating a mangel-wurzel! But seriously, old lad, there is something to be said for your position: it may be the "hell on wheels" you say it is, but you have avoided Active Service. Indeed, how you have managed to hibernate at that college for two whole years is a mystery to me. I think you've done extraordinarily well, and I'm sure any G.I. just back from Okinawa would agree with me.

You also say you may be out of it altogether in a year. Great news! Also, that a trip to England is a practical possibility. Remember you have a standing invitation to stay at our humble mansion for as long as you like. At my end, the demob news is all rather vague. My own number is depressingly high; in fact, it was only last week that, for the first time in my Army career, I discovered a chap with a higher one! Never mind: I will be out within a year myself— you'll see! Though I have no grounds for this prediction other than the Lewis determination.

P.S. Have just received a rejection slip from 'Victory' for some cartoons I sent them, including the Attwood masterpiece. Too subtle, I suppose.


September 2nd 1945

Courtney old lad,

As I write these lines I am reclining in a cushioned armchair, dulcet melodies of Brahms floating over the radio in proximity. I recall that a year ago it was a different story when Desmond and I were making desperate plans to desert from the Ballykinlar concentration camp. He — capable of withstanding any physical or mental rigours — was only doing it for adventure, while my own motive was simply to avert an impending breakdown. As I reach for a glass of port and my copy of Somerset Maugham, I wonder how the old boy is getting along?

Speaking of Brahms; although I don't think I mentioned it at the time, Wilbur and I met a budding musician on the boat — a young pianist who was coming over here on a concert tour. He is up here at Razmak now, and gave a recital earlier this evening in the Church Hall, during which I sketched him. He is very withdrawn, totally absorbed in his work and difficult to talk to. All the same, I tackled him afterwards about some of my pet problems: for instance, is there such a thing as humorous music in the same way as there is humorous art and prose? He mentioned Rossini whose work I don't know, never having paid attention to much more than Tchaikowsky's 'Nutcracker'. Not that I would not wish to broaden my horizon given the opportunity; and I'm painfully aware that at the venerable age of nineteen I have plenty of time to do so. If I remain here for the next few months I should be able to make a few preliminary excursions into this field.

You know, living as I am in what can only be called spiritually sterile surroundings has enhanced rather than weakened my aesthetic sense as well as my general intellectual awareness. One might have expected the reverse to be true, but the value of these things is plainer to see by way of contrast. When one is deprived of something it becomes intrinsically more precious.

There are times, Courtney, when I become overwhelmed by nausea at the incorrigible lack of spirituality in my fellow men! I feel like bursting with despair! (No apologies for this outburst, old lad, as I'm sure you must feel the same sometimes.) Officers — men; Indians — British; all are equally shallow: insects existing within the circumscribed field of their daily routine, treating each other according to his position in the system. Individuality they have none; their identity being indistinguishable from what they *do*. To me this is a bee hive — an ant's nest, and I cannot accept it! Shaw put it like this somewhere: "It's not what you do, it's what you are that counts." This is why I can break their rules — be flippant, irresponsible, and disrespectful without losing any of my own self-respect.

Well, to come back to earth, the latest news is that I am once more the slave of the bed-pan and clinical thermometer — not to mention the penicillin squeezer and enema tube! In short, I am back on ward duty, but this time looking after the officers. My duties dispensing health to these select patients leads me to record the following observations which may, or may not, be illuminating: the British e.b. usually arrives on a stretcher having fallen off a horse or having been bitten in the leg by a rapacious jackal. When I take his temperature, he never wipes the thermometer before it goes into his mouth.

The Indian officer, on the other hand, invariably comes in with scabies of dysentery, and when I produce my thermometer he always wipes it!

Only one Indian officer in residence at present. This morning I sauntered nonchalantly into his room to find him crouching in the middle of the floor incanting the magic words, "Allah! Allah!" Having completely exhausted himself doing what to my casual eye appeared to be Swedish exercises, he staggered to his bed and collapsed. I was not surprised to find he had a temperature of 104°. Whether this display was simply the usual matutinal observances practised by Muslims or something special on account of his illness, I don't know; but I gave him the prescribed potion and told him not to do it again.

September 9th 1945

A lively week on the ward, old lad: fraught with divers humorous incidents, one might say. I've not exactly killed one of my patients yet, but feel that the disaster might befall at any moment.

Take last Tuesday. Inadvertently administered the wrong pills to a lieutenant: not a high-ranking officer, so a minor solecism, I thought. Yet when the doctor heard about it he singularly failed to collapse in a fit of hysterics as I had hoped he would. Laugh it off is always my watchword. My colleagues, on the other hand, think my blunders are frightfully amusing. There was the day when I put methylated spirit into the gargle. (God knows how this happened!) The result being that my reputation on the wards as a comedian soared to new heights. Whereas the doctors were none too pleased, on my home ground I was feted as a hero!

Wednesday. While making my early rounds I discovered Capt. Hardy was A.W.O.L. Capt. Hardy, by the way, is a wild though amiable Australian who had been brought in under armed escort. Among other things, one of his problems was an ungovernable urge for drink, and there had been great consternation earlier when a bottle of gin had been discovered under his pillow during an inspection by some high-ranking big-wig. Anyway, the gallant Captain had seemingly decamped during the night as he had left a note pinned to his chart stating simply, "Feel fine. Toodle-oo! Thanks for the medicine." Dashed amusing, in my view, but once again the M.O. failed to collapse with a laughing fit. No sense of humour, this man, Courtney: none at all. An absolute necessity for a doctor, I should have thought, especially if he is relying on me to administer the treatment.

Friday started off well. I inadvertently put a bandage on the wrong man and had him sitting in the garden before realizing my mistake. Lack of concentration or something. Then there was the stretcher case. I dropped the darned thing — the stretcher, trying to get it out of the ambulance, and there was this officer hopping about in the road in his pyjamas! For an acute case of amoebic dysentery he seemed very active and his vocal chords had not been impaired.

In my sober moments, Courtney, I am bound to admit that despite my gentle sympathetic nature, I am really not cut out for this job. In matters of life and death I am hopelessly incompetent. How my first case — the Ghurka with the gastric ulcer, pulled through I shall never know. But he did and the first sign of his recovery, I recall, was when he asked for his famous chopper, like a child wanting its teddy bear. It struck me at the time that it's the job of the R.A.M.C. up here to patch up these ruffians, let them out, and then get the beds ready for their next victims! By and large a futile occupation, which perhaps does something to explain why I am inclined to take my duties lightly.

Which brings me up to Saturday. A sad day indeed. Yes, old lad, yesterday we all attended a military funeral, though not I hasten to add of one of my patients! The poor devil had fallen in battle, the local brigands having shot their first Britisher since my arrival. An occasion of great solemnity, on which sombre note I close this missive.

P.S. A letter from Aunt Edna today enclosing a news cutting. Her vigilant optic had spotted the latest on P.G.W., namely that he is planning to go to England taking his war work with him: five novels and a play, all written during internment. Three cheers for P.G.! Also another one for Auntie!

September 22nd 1945

Courtney old stickleback,

You may or may not have heard of a lively little comic-strip for infants which appears every morning in the Daily Express. It is entitled, 'The Adventures of Rupert the Bear', and recounts with much detail how this poor little animal is kept constantly on the move, unremittingly persecuted by a malignant Providence. I mention this because it occurs to me that myself and Rupert have much in common. At which point you will have guessed that I am being posted again!

Yes, old lad, the glad tidings came in the form of a telegram from the Depot signed by my old mentor the Major, now promoted to Lieutenant Colonel. I am to report there at once, though as an epidemic of infantile paralysis has just been declared here, the trip has been postponed for another ten days.

It is now abundantly clear that I am destined to be a roamer. When I came to Razmak I thought I had found my niche, but this has proved a delusion. I now see that the best I can hope for is a few months respite between postings. What a life, laddie! Is it surprising that I am constitutionally incapable of taking my episodic career seriously? One may be here with one lot of blokes one week and gone the next, heading for another lot. If the Army has taught me anything, it is the Buddhist axiom that all outward material things are transient and should never be relied on. Somerset Maugham is also inclined to this school of thought, as I expect you have noticed.

So here I am again, poised for yet another tortuous trek back to the dear old Depot where I shall be buffeted, bounced and branded, denuded of hair and dispatched to 'blank'. As this is no idle posting but part of some sinister scheme, I am somewhat disquieted; however, I shall keep you well-informed of the sequence of events. One thing I can say with certainty, when I get back to Deolali I will do my utmost to pick up the elusive threads which Wilbur will have left behind him. I have not heard from him for months.

Well, old lad, back to the jaws of purgatory! Keep your eyes peeled for a likely-looking caravan.

October 7th 1945

Courtney old lad,

Just a few lines en route to the old hell-hole. Am writing this at the Sandes Home, Rawalpindi, where I stopped on the way up, if you remember. The journey is such a long one that I calculate we can loaf, gorge, and sleep hoggishly here for four days without precipitating any awkward questions at the other end. The place is run by two elderly English ladies who would not be out of place taking the air at Eastbourne; consequently it is markedly reminiscent of an English hotel.

So far, the journey has been no ordeal; in fact, enjoyable. The drive down the winding mountain trail to Bannu at breakneck speed was a superlative blend of thrills and scenic grandeur. More optical orgies around Marindus: the jagged mountains set against a glorious sunset were a splendid sight, though my travelling companion characteristically averred that he would "rather see London by gaslight any time."! The Sind desert, by the way, has cooled off considerably since June.

Have reached Delhi without mishap, though very short of money due to our sojourn at Rawalpindi: only ten rupees to finance the remaining four days of the trip. Am in the Wavell Canteen where I have just polished off a meal of liver, onions, and ice-cream, plus a monumental milk shake which should keep me going till tomorrow.

We were held up at Rawalpindi till Thursday morning having failed to get berths on the night train. Spent a rough night on a board at the inaptly named 'rest camp' nearby. . . More fairyland scenery approaching Delhi: the jungle resplendent in the dawn is rich with exotic bird life.

I have been trying to read a novel by John Buchan but found I was far less bored doing nothing. Apart from being an irritating empire-builder, he has no sense of humour, and in a moment of exasperation I threw the book out of the window.



Have been back at the Depot five days, spent mainly in loafing and skipping parades. Under the sobriquet of A. B. Brocklebank I am taking things easy.

I see from the notice-board that I am off to an unknown destination tomorrow with a formidable contingent of wart-hogs. The sooner the better, is how I look at it, as Deolali without Wilbur or Desmond is insufferable: a hot-bed of discipline which I cannot endure as I uncompromisingly refuse to be made into a peace-time soldier.

All this, however, is something of a digression as I was about to announce that your latest much battle-scarred missive lies before me. The one mailed on August 18th. The Lewis tonic mixture which I am administering in liberal doses seems to be having an effect as this one was much more lighthearted in tone.

Am elated to hear that you endorse my Square Peg Club

brainwave, and wholeheartedly agree to your suggested symbol, ⬤ which will look fine embossed in purple on blue notepaper!

As to your bewildered comment on the British general election. . . "What's the matter with that fat-headed country of yours?" you say. One has to know the psychology of the fat-headed British wart-hog before attempting an explanation.

As you know, I am not a Churchill supporter, other than as a caricaturist; I think his replacement by the rabbit-faced Attlee is bound to weaken the ancient art of the political cartoon. On the other hand, given the hypothesis that the war was worth fighting, it is undeniable that Churchill contributed greatly to the winning of it. To topple him from power in the moment of national triumph must therefore be accounted, not only ungracious, but unpatriotic.

Assuming that political power through the ballot box is held by the working man in present-day Britain, what then is his political thinking? The main thing to remember, old lad, is that he hasn't any — he is governed by instinct. From my front-line vantage point as a private soldier I can say unequivocally that the wart-hog's chief political instinct is to live as untrammelled by governmental control as possible. He hates authority — any authority, and will always vote against it when invited to do so. Barrack-room conversation, for instance, consists of a continual grousing against everybody in the Army above the rank of corporal, with particular animosity expended at Monty or whatever general is in supreme command. On the home front, the king pin at the head of the government is their main target, being held to be chiefly responsible for their heart-felt grievances. And this is the point, old lad; the wart-hog is always seething with grievances — he is forever complaining that he is being given the dirty end of the stick. So you see it was to be expected, following the miseries he has suffered in the war, that given the opportunity, he would give Churchill a good swift kick in the seat of his pants! Not that I believe Attlee, despite his socialism, will win any more favour. It's like a game of musical chairs with the various parties moving round in circles. I predict a Tory revival in the not too distant future and a Liberal come-back sooner or later!

If all this sounds too scathing, I should add that I think a cynical attitude to government is justified to some extent. A general election is something of a charade: a contest of distorted facts and rash promises to see who shall win the exalted positions at stake. I deliberately don't use the word 'power' because governments in a democracy control very little; like the rest of us, they are swept along on a current of events.

To turn to other things. One of my first acts upon arriving here last Sunday was to saunter down to the hospital in search of news about Wilbur. Some of his acquaintances were still there, and this is the tale told to me by a communicative corporal. . . You remember that he was working for a psychiatrist at the time. Well, he was ordered to escort a patient to Poona which he did, afterwards deciding to pop down to Bombay, a mere hundred miles, and take a look round before returning home to roost. What occurred in Bombay — a place where anything can happen — is not quite clear, but having committed a number of misdemeanours, Wilbur was placed under arrest and sent back to Deolali to face a court martial. I gather his C.O. had been in Bombay at the time. Knowing Wilbur, I think he could be relied upon to play up once he saw which way the wind was blowing, and I can visualize him appearing before the judges wearing his well-known yachting cap, and that sort of thing. What the sentence was is unclear: what isn't unclear is that he refused to accept it and promptly perpetrated a number of insubordinate acts; one of which, reputedly, is that he demolished a piano with a hatchet! I know myself that there is an unruly streak in Wilbur: there was the occasion back in June when he nearly went berserk with a table knife. It was in a canteen: he was feeling out-of-sorts and had ordered a cool salad. When the bearer arrived with a plate of liver and fried bread something seemed to snap in his brain, as they say, and he very nearly attacked the wretched man. He threatened to slit his throat, as a matter of fact, though I think myself it was ninety-five per cent histrionics.

Be that as it may, the upshot on this occasion, so I am told, was that the hospital psychiatrist suddenly found that he had lost a secretary and gained a patient! And to cut a long story short, Wilbur was promptly repatriated and is now out of the Army! There is much in this yarn that requires elucidation, and there may of course be inaccurate details. The full story, old lad, can only be recounted by the man himself.

(Later)

Have met my old pal the Adjutant again, and we parted the best of friends!

Resultant of a tiff with a particularly bone-headed sergeant I found myself on some absurd charge this afternoon: failing to observe draft procedure as posted on the camp notice-board, or something equally puerile. My actual words to the Adj. when invited to speak before sentence was passed, were: "I admit my mistake, sir. I just consider this court scene to be unwarrantable." Whereupon he dismissed the case with a light laugh, and I have never seen a sergeant turn a more profuse shade of magenta!

I shall shortly be on my way to a spot near Poona, and from what I have seen of my new comrades, they are a very motley crew indeed.

*Saturday, October 20th 1945*

Well, well, well, boys and girls, another Ballykinlar!! From the graveyard atmosphere to the swaggering empire-builders with fiery red moustaches, this desert dump is reminiscent of the old hell-hole! My suspicion that the Army has not yet realized the war is over and is going to carry on playing soldiers is now confirmed. I suppose I had to end up in a battle unit sooner or later, which being so, No. 6 British Field Ambulance is as good (or as bad) as any other. As I say, they appear to take things seriously so friction will ensue.

More anon.

October 31st 1945

Courney old lad,

In starting, I'd like to apologize for the 'ink vicissitude'. The old Lewis pen has been ailing of late, so I had it overhauled by the local vet. I have been scribbling badinage with it since 1941 and I was not surprised when the man extracted what looked like a dried orange pip from the feed-duct. In broken English, this turbaned Indian explained to me the fallacy of using water-proof ink mixed with Nitric acid. Now, I maintain that the individual should mix his ink, as his cocktail, to his own taste. But as the necessary purple ingredients are improcurable at the moment, I shall have to resort to conventional Swan. However, despite the dreary colour, you may rest assured that I am using the same old nib (pen-point in your vernacular) that wrote our two stories, plus the clip, feed-duct, and sucking tube that you know so well.

Well, laddie, I got your latest on Friday, and this is great news indeed. Your entire letter reflects elation at your impending emancipation from the binding chains and weighty balls. I will tell you straight, Courtney, I believe the armed forces to be an essentially evil institution: it is founded on primitive principles and it flourishes on hatred. It aims at turning men into mindless robots by annihilating all individualism. That you have managed to see the war out from the inside of a college is indeed a triumph, as I think I have mentioned before.

As for me, since arriving at this miserable dump ten days ago, apart from nearly killing myself trying to put up

81

tents (there are very few buildings), all I have seen is the inside of the cook house. I have noticed that if there is anybody intellectually inclined about, he usually gravitates into this sweat-shop. And looking on the bright side, I am bound to admit that peeling half a hundred-weight of potatoes does assist thought. Many are the days I have spent scrubbing tiled floors with Desmond or Wilbur!

At present I am on mess duty, condemned to feed the hungry wart-hog his daily ration of bully-beef and swamp-water pickle! And I feel I can't close this paragraph without a mention of the delicious cheese concoction they all had for lunch. To quote one of my fellow slaves: "A layer of rice, a layer of cheese, and a layer of soot."!

No doubt it will break the rules to divulge that the destination of this outfit is said to be China; a rumour which appears substantiated by the lecture on Hong Kong we attended the other day. I have no objection to seeing the world, though naturally I would prefer to do so under my own steam and in different company. As for Hong Kong, I wouldn't choose it for a holiday as it seems to be infested with pirates, gorillas, and prostitutes, as well as being prone to typhoons. On the other hand, it must be an improvement on this place.

Our Company Officer also thinks we are headed for China. "Ho!" he said amiably as I stood before his desk this morning. (He has, by the way, a lovely bushy moustache — the standard military ginger.) "I hear you are an artist browned off with the Army?" I didn't deny the charge; as you know, I spend my life promoting this image. "Well," he went on, "How would you like to teach the lads Art when we all get to China?"

For the moment this had me nonplussed, as you may well imagine. For one thing, I know nothing about teaching art — Chinese or otherwise, and for another, I couldn't quite see the point of the assignment. I pointed out that it was my considered opinion that it would be impossible to teach wart-hogs fine art in China or anywhere else. But as he remained adamant and I could not see any harm in the idea which suggested the possibility of another sinecure like the one I had at the Depot, I accepted the proposal. Whether it will come to anything remains to be seen.

I have a feeling that China won't be as hot as India or as depressing. Everywhere I go in the land of the Maharajahs there is squalor and apathy. The bullock cart seems to symbolize the place, and ought to be depicted in outline on the national flag: a sort of somnolent plodding along in a chronic state of lethargy. The drive and ambition that has thrown up western civilization is absent here — due mainly, I suspect, to the climate. A listless negative attitude prevails; an attitude that is reflected in Hindu thought. One of their gurus has put it this way: 'Civilization is like a circular running track: the runners expend a lot of energy but get nowhere.'

Now, I concede his point as far as the Army is concerned; in fact, I have made the same observation myself. A fanatical obsession with desultory pursuits is the rock on which the whole lunatic edifice is founded. But even for an indolent chap like myself, the Indian view is far too supine. I mean, I have never supported the slothful do-nothing philosophy, have I? One must strive to create something; art, literature — something valuable. I have never been a nihilist.

Speaking of Art: my chances of seeing 'The Picture of Dorian Gray' are negligible, I fear. But following your effusive encomiums I will do so if the film is shown within ten miles of the camp. Sounds something special, as it should be with George Sanders speaking Oscar Wilde's lines. Criticizing Sanders is — as the Observer said about Wodehouse — like taking a spade to a soufflé. The film will have to be very good to restore my flagging faith in the movie industry. We have a camp cinema, of course, (called the Visapur Talkies!) but I have seen some pretty deadly stuff lately — largely for distraction. Saw Chas. Laughton pull some more facial expressions last night in some worthless show.

Back to the cook house. . .

Courtney old lad,

Cast your monocled optic over any daily tabloid at the present time, and you will see such inspiring headlines as: 'Commando Strike In Pong-Ping. General Wagflag's Ultimatum To North Borneo'. Not to mince words, old lad, the British empire-builder is sticking his be-gumboiled neck out all over the Far Eastern map!

Now, don't misunderstand me: I may deplore the habit but, at the same time, I have the perspicacity to realize that it can't be stopped. A glance down the gory annals of English history will make it abundantly plain that the noble sport of taking on the local natives with a view to unfurling the Union Jack at a spot where the sun never sets has been pursued — possibly since the days of King Alfred (ignoring for this discussion the reign of Aethelred-the-Unready). My complaint, you see, is not so much that these martial exploits occur; it is that I am expected to take part in them! I have fair reason to suppose that the British e.b. has such an incorrigibly one-track mind that he is mentally incapable of formulating the concept that somebody somewhere of soldiering age might not be bursting with eagerness to rally to the colours and do his bit in promoting these adventures. To put it in a nutshell, laddie, the strenuous efforts I have been making have so far failed to convince the authorities that Private G. Lewis is unsuited to be a member of No. 6. British Field Ambulance, South East Asia Command. And believe me, I have been trying my utmost the last three weeks.

To start with, the Hong Kong lark is off (all that nonsense about art classes): we have been told to prepare ourselves for 'police duties in the South Pacific'. At present there's 'a bit of sport' going on in Java, and rumour has it that this is our destination. Whatever it is we are being trained to do, you can be certain of one thing — we'll do it the hard way. Swimming ashore wearing full kit at one a.m. in a hail of bullets, or I don't know the Company Officer. I've seen the look in his eye.

No. 6. F.A., let me tell you, is part of the 2nd Division (the famous Fighting 2nd Division), and if I ever get to where it's all happening, I expect we will find ourselves fully-stretched picking up the corpses! Not, I hasten to add, that I have any intention of getting there. I have already told you my feelings of reluctance in being a peace-time soldier; they are even stronger than my reluctance in being made a wartime soldier. Picture me, at the moment, as a punch ball being incessantly battered by a bunch of N.C.O.s wearing knuckledusters, and you have a graphic image of the situation. I would draw the cartoon for you myself, old lad, but I am not up to it just now. Too punch drunk. . .

Spiritually I am strong enough to take on the lot, but the joust is taking its toll of my nerves and physique. (This letter, quite honestly, is a sort of therapy.) On the credit side, I have gained a reputation far and wide as a loony crackpot of an artist and the despair of the battalion!

As usual, the Sergeant-major is my chief antagonist: it did not take his beady eye long to pick me out. I forget what the charge was for — something absurd. But I got seven days, and the gloves were off. Once you have been 'blooded', so to speak, you are a marked man. Incidentally, the C.O. was particularly censorious about the officer's cap badge which I have been wearing without reproof for over a year now. Comment here on the mentality of men who spend their day punctiliously scrutinizing cap badges is superfluous.

Well, after a week of 'fatigues' under the iron heels of my tormentors I was feeling decidedly enervated; but I suppose I was lucky to complete the stretch before the training programme started on the 12th. This began in grand Ballykinlar style with a vigorous two mile trot with the S.M. puffing along in front looking like an angry hippopotamus. Obviously the word had gone out from Brigade h.q. that the new arrivals had got to be toughened up before their coming assault on the South Pacific.

For the whole week the order has been boots, shorts, and bare chests. As if sun-scorched torsos were not enough,

Whisky Whiskers the C.O. also proclaimed the desirability of hard feet, and to show he meant it, took us for a strenuous ramble amidst the rocky hills in the full heat of the day. When I wandered off at one point he was most upset. I was pretty exhausted — and probably looked it, otherwise it would assuredly have meant more than a reprimand.

The next morning, owing to stiffness in the knees following the previous day's romp plus a general feeling of lassitude, I failed to keep step on parade. The upshot: fifteen minutes solitary drill under the R.S.M., during which he remarked among other things — "My boy, you'll learn!" I had certainly learnt that it is a mistake to try to harden the feet in a hurry.

I can't believe that it was sheer chance that, after a full day's training, they picked me for all-night guard duty yesterday. One has to patrol the camp looking for stray dogs and cobras: a somewhat tedious pursuit as there aren't any. When I rang up the Colonel for some lamp oil (you can't spot the cobra without a light, after all), I thought I might hear more about the incident this morning. I did — from the R.S.M.'s own rose-petal lips. My main impression — that he was somewhat peeved. Even if I tried, nothing I could do would mollify him; so why bother? There is a mutual antipathy between G.L. and these men. If there wasn't, I'd lose all my self-respect.

*November 17th*

Things are moving. One of the companies has gone, and Whisky Whiskers' 'shirts-off' scheme has dissolved. We are now performing clearing up and maintenance duties around the deserted camp, and — get this! — I have been recruited as a policeman!

*November 28th*

Still playing at soldiers, but there's time for other things as well. Nothing to read at the moment, so naturally I have been dropping in to the Visapur Talkies whenever possible for escape. Have seen some lousy films, to be honest; the lousiest being 'Keep Your Powder Dry', the outright winner of the Golden Corn Cob for 1945. However, all these flops have been more than offset by Walt Disney's latest cartoon extravaganza, 'The Three Caballeros'. Now, I readily concede that the contrast between the fantasy world of Walt Disney and my present sordid and demoralizing situation is bound to cloud my judgement somewhat, weighting it heavily in favour of Disney. And the contrast, I need hardly tell you, is pretty terrific. It is as if the artist, after a shuddering look at a demented war-torn world, had impounded himself in one of his own creation, producing this film which he had then thrown out into the darkness to explode in a dazzling display of colour, jubilance, humour, melody, and song. It is an affirmation, Courtney; an affirmation of beauty and gaiety amidst a world engulfed in the sombre ugliness of war. I emerged from the tatty picture house spiritually revitalized, dazed yet ecstatic; and even the spectacle of a bunch of miserable Indian wart-hogs amusing themselves by breaking sticks across the backs of some donkeys was powerless to dispel it. I went to see it again the following night and appreciated it more than ever.

Just heard that some wild over-night escapade planned for this evening has been called off due to a riot breaking out among the local natives. Hats off to the golly-wogs! Long may they skirmish!

*Sunday, December 2nd 1945*

It would take more than a local rebellion to disrupt our training programme. The wild over-night escapade duly transpired one day later. After a rough ride along almost non-existent roads, we were finally deposited somewhere in the Indian landscape — by far the most beautiful place I have seen since I came here. Trees and tropical foliage; purple mountains in the middle-distance; two lazy white bullocks walking gently round in circles drawing water from a well. An idyllic peaceful picture where one could rest and restore one's tattered nerves. . . Not a bit of it! The moment the Army descended all was jangling chaos. The morning was spent strenuously erecting tents; upon the completion of which came the order to take them down! As usual, nobody seemed to know why we were there, what we were supposed to be doing, or where we were going. And quite frankly, now that it's all over and done with, I still don't know why we were there, what we were doing, or where we went. All I can say for certain is that the wallah who was working the bullocks must have thought we were bloody mad!

Frankly, my enthusiasm for the game of cowboys and Indians waned some years ago, and Whisky Whiskers' noctural belly-crawling escapade left me quite, quite cold. Being jolted about for hours in the back of that tin wagon made me feel ill, and I reported same to the R.S.M. who was surprisingly kindly. I suppose I must have looked ill otherwise he would have bitten my head off. The next morning found me almost immovable and with a splitting headache. Yet within hours I was ordered back to the old cook house for pickle dishing. I tell you, laddie, if there's to be much more of this carry on, I've had it. . .

(Later)

The news has just broken that the expected jaunt to the Javanese jungles begins at dawn tomorrow, which means I had better steel myself for the usual programme of panics, postponements, and organized chaos: the time-worn method by which the British bulldog muddles through. They have issued each man with a revolver for this trip. A bit rash, as I could trust any of this outfit (myself included) to injure himself with a tin opener.

Well, old lad, I must get this long letter posted before we leave. As usual my watch-word is 'Relax or go scatty' and 'Copy the cat' (the one at Boyce, remember?).

P.S. Sorry to read about Robert Benchley's demise. (On a scrap of newspaper in the bogs actually.) This world needs all the humorists it can get.

P.P.S. Just heard the big exodus has been postponed for forty-eight hours!

December 16th 1945

Courtney old lad,

It's a fortnight since I wrote you, and I can say without exaggeration that it has been a fortnight replete with astonishing events. Now that the action has been shot, so to speak, at last I am able to sit down and outline the scenario.

First and foremost, I am happy to tell you that I have managed to extricate myself from that gang of lunatics that comprise No. 6. Field Ambulance. They are now on a ship going God-knows where to do God-knows what; though I am certain that whatever it is they are going to do, it will be a criminal waste of time and money and will probably turn the saner elements amongst them into slavering imbeciles.

Be that as it may, they deemed my presence so undesirable that on the very eve of departure, they hoofed me and another bloke whom they mistakenly considered my side-kick back to dear old Deolali. The sanest act, in my view, they will ever commit. So you can see, old lad, that my recalcitrance paid off in the end, in addition to its spiritual benefits.

As I say, the very eve of departure, and also the eve of my twentieth birthday! I had actually stacked my kit on the lorry when the dispatch rider rolled up, and the S.M. after a baffled look at the papers, gave me his final order (in almost a deferential tone, I thought) which was to take it off again. Accompanied by the Canadian bloke, I spent the night on guard duty and so watched the dawn break on my twenty-first year. I felt it was a happy augury, and I made a silent prayer that when I celebrated my next birthday I

89

would be home again and free from the fetters and shackles.

By breakfast time we had the camp to ourselves, and I spent the rest of the day lying on my charpoy and reading some of the letters and literature that had arrived in a batch two days earlier. A happy birthday indeed! And all the more so because it was so completely unexpected. The peace and tranquillity of the deserted camp was ineffable. Gone was all the senseless bustle, and irate yelps from sergeant-majors no longer disturbed the soporific Indian air. Within hours, donkeys, birds, and other wild life had ventured into the camp and were quietly browsing.

One reason why the powers-that-be may have linked myself and the Canadian is that we shared the same tent. He is a genial guy with a sense of humour whose main fault, apart from a delusion that he is as funny as Bog Hope, is that he thinks he could double for Humphrey Bogart. He used to chafe me a lot: "I get a kick out of you, Lewis; you horrible specimen!" and that sort of thing. Not exactly an endearing character, but I wish him luck.

Anyway, we duly repaired to Deolali last Wednesday, and you should have seen the Adjutant's face when he saw me milling around the office. His mouth sagged open, important papers slipped from between limp fingers, and he just gazed at me pop-eyed. Having recovered his equilibrium, he beckoned me into his office, and after a friendly chit-chat asked me to name any job I would like to try. Well, I had been thinking about this and I had fixed my sights on Poona. Poona — the empire-builder's citadel. I had decided no tour of the British Raj would be complete without a visit. In addition to this line of thought, there was the paramount necessity of assuming a sedentary posture for a spell after the stress and strain of the past two months. I knew Poona was the centre for laboratory training, and while a wooden stool is not an arm-chair, at least you can sit on it. When I broached this idea to the Adj. he pounced on it eagerly and said he would gladly send me to Poona for good! But knowing my record, if I was marooned on Robinson Crusoe's desert island, I don't suppose I would stay there long.

So here I am, off to Poona tomorrow! This lab course commences after Christmas, and if it comes to nothing, I shall at least have put in four more months under salubrious conditions.

I have been lucky, Courtney — damned lucky. I can only put it down to a benign providence and the fact that I spared no pains to make it clear to my task-masters that Graham Lewis was indisputably unsuited to be a tool in the hands of British empire-builders.

It is time I made a declaration. If a choice had to be made, I would unhesitatingly put myself on the side of the wart-hog in preference to joining the other group. The empire-builder is the greater menace, old lad, the greater menace by far. (In a sense, I made this choice when I chucked up the commission course at Ganges; a move which I never regretted.) The wart-hog, you see, is merely the tool who is grudgingly compelled to carry out the e.b.'s aggressive aims. Like myself, he is forced to bear the yoke and pull the imperial cart; and as such, I commiserate with him. This explains the undoubted acclaim my recalcitrance was accorded among the men of the field unit. They used to call me The Colonel, you know, because I always wear an officer's beret. It also explains why the authorities had to get rid of me: my presence was too demoralizing.

On the few occasions lately when I have cast an eye down the columns of a newspaper I have been struck by the devastating effects of the war. We may indeed have achieved victory, but what has been the price? It is quite obvious that Britain is no longer Great, in the sense of being a great power. Without Lend Lease we would not have been able to carry on the war, and when Truman suddenly stopped this last summer, the parlous state of the British economy was at once revealed. Needless to say, the pride of the British e.b. was wounded to the quick. My own feeling is that this turn of events could lead to the nation's salvation as in a crippled Britain the sun would rapidly set on the Empire, and the empire-builder, along with his lunatic philosophy of aggrandisement and exploitation, would fade from the scene of history. Britain could well be left on a par with Switzerland, and might become a salubrious place to live in by directing its energies towards the Arts and Crafts with Sport as a safety-valve for the competitive instincts.

If this vision fails to materialize I shall seriously have to consider assuming a false name and going to live in Zululand. But is Zululand safe? It has just crossed my mind that it is probably a British Protectorate!

*December 24th 1945*

I am writing this by the light of a full moon. As expected I reached Poona a week ago, and by and large, I am happy to report the horizon looks brighter at last. Although the town is a little unctuous for my liking with a lot of stern purposeful men dashing about muttering numbers, it appears to be much more civilized than other settlements: less in the way of smells, pregnant goats, etc. It will do for the nonce.

Until this course commences I am working on a ward the size of Paddington Station, and am bored to distraction. The one thing worthy of mention, perhaps, is that I have run into a friendly chap I knew at Moston (name of Eddie: I may have mentioned him). So at least I have someone to talk to.

Tomorrow is Christmas Day, but the seasonal magic is somewhat vitiated by the fact that the weather is like mid-summer here. Also by the fact that I have been put on fire picket tonight. The same thing happened last year at Moston, I remember. Irrespective of the climate, the wards have been decorated in the good old English style with fir trees, lots of cotton wool, and festoons of coloured bandages fastened to the walls with sticking plaster. So when I need a dressing I merely pluck down a snow-ball!

Well, old lad, that's it for the present: I must bring this lengthy missive to a close. Tomorrow I shall imbibe a silent, solitary toast to our mutual emancipation, utilizing the bottle of Australian port I bought back at Razmak and

92

which I always carry with me in my large pack.
I see it is now past midnight, so

A happy Christmas!

Graham

# PART TWO

Courtney old lad,

Your first letter since October reached me last Friday. I make no remonstrations. I just hope your indolence preys on your conscience!

So you don't get out till November? Naturally, you have my sympathy. If it's any consolation, this is the earliest date I myself can hope for release.

The lab course is quite tolerable, though how long I can pretend to be interested in bio-chemistry remains to be seen. Naturally, I presented myself at the preliminary interview as being hellishly keen. As usual there are the precocious youths who lap up the agenda like a cat does milk whilst I labour silently and abortively in the background. But this doesn't worry me. There is no point in my putting my shoulder to the wheel in an attempt to pass this course, as assuming I did, the most likely upshot would be a posting to Siam for window-washing duties!

I had the class in convulsions this morning having drawn an assortment of comical germs — some of them smoking pipes, across the pages of my notebook. Also an elaborate Heath Robinson machine designed for catching them. The officiating captain was mildly amused, I thought.

Since I last wrote, my tottering physique has improved somewhat though I have this chronic feeling of lassitude. Perhaps it's the sultry weather or the low state of my red corpuscles? I don't know. . . Smallpox is ravaging the district at present, which means I shall probably go down with mumps!

Heretofore, I don't think I have mentioned that whilst in the field unit I knew a colourful individual, an ex-paratrooper who said that before the war he had been a wall-of-death rider with a fun fair. The only kick he can get out of life is by cheating death executing some daredevil stunt or other. Anyway, he was released from my old graveyard because he is subject to sudden brain seizures resulting from a motor cycle accident, and I met him again a few days ago in Poona. He is lodging in the nut ward here at the hospital, but is allowed out as he is not thought to be a public menace. He is quite a mild-mannered bloke actually, though a trifle impulsive. We pottered round the bookstalls for an hour or so. He told me about the smash which nearly killed him. When he came to his senses and found his leg almost ripped off, he said he started to hunt around the ditch looking for his missing knee-cap!


January 25th

Collapsed two days ago: all my faculties on strike. Was diagnosed as having acute bronchitis and excused all duties. But aided by a liberal supply of pills and lozenges, I seem to be pulling through. I see I shall have to humour the Lewis shell. The wear and tear of Active Service is beginning to take its toll.


Sunday, February 17th

My apologies, old lad. I should have posted this weeks ago but don't seem to be able to get it finished. Fact is I have been working on a serious essay — an exposition of my views on life, with special reference to the moral and political shortcomings of the British empire-builder. A veritable gusher of sagacity and humour, I assure you, and lovingly dedicated to the distinguished members of the Square Peg Club. I shall get copies typed out at the earliest opportunity.

Well, tomorrow is Der Tag, the day I am due to take the first Lab exam. And I confess, old lad, that my never very intense interest in aglutinations, molecular weights, and the staphlococci microbe broke down completely some time ago. The onslaught was too great. So it looks as if my days here are numbered and that I shall very soon be guilty of that lamentable solecism — the 'when I was in Poona' habit!

98

I am so sure of the result of this test that I even refused to pose with the rest of the class for a group photo that was being taken. I suppose this minor act of rebellion has not improved my chances, but who cares! In certain moods I can be very hidebound, and the regimentalism behind this photo scheme was really too absurd.

I am bored with the whole shooting match, Courtney — bored to the eyebrows! Demob creeps on at such a snail's pace that I am seriously thinking of following in Wilbur's hallowed footsteps and getting discharged from the Army as a nut case. A simple matter: I would just shove my essay in front of a psychiatrist and wait for the attendants to come along with a straight-jacket! Wilbur, incidentally, was discharged from the forces at Birmingham at the end of last year. I have this from a fairly reliable source here. For some inexplicable reason I have not heard from the old lad since last August.

Now, regarding the enclosed photograph. . . I trust it *is* enclosed, and has not been purloined by a predatory censor *en route*. In case it has been, I am referring to a picture of a wise-looking bird sucking dispassionately at a briar pipe and making doodles on the December issue of Strand magazine. His name is Vere; at least, that is one of several names he possesses — the one in current use. And he is the author of the delightful literary *jeu d'esprit* also enclosed: the 'Dissertation on Eggs'. When you have read this, old lad, I am sure you will be as convinced as I am that there is only one place for such a distinguished individual as this, and that is the Square Peg Club.

Now I imagine that at this moment, Courtney, you are fingering your esteemed monocle rather irritably as I recall your remark from an earlier letter, "I suggest we limit the membership to four, Graham." But, laddie, it simply can't be done. The world is but sparsely populated with freaks of our kidney, and like the Salvation Army, the Square Peg Club must turn none away from its protecting portals.

I hasten to add that there is no question of the membership eventually wending its way down Piccadilly two-by-two in a crocodile, or pushing into the Albert Hall in their thousands to attend the annual dinner. Perish the thought, old lad! But I do think we must treat any candidate on his merits rather than adhere to some preconsidered policy. Now, when I broached the idea of the Club to Vere after a month's careful observation he almost burst out of his collar with delight. He had never thought of such a thing and was captivated by the idea; a sure sign, in my view, of his eligibility. Again, when I showed him your photograph, 'On the wings of Thought', I got another favourable reaction. "Good," he said. "He doesn't wear sock suspenders." He also suggested that P.G.W. should be elected as an Honorary Member, which I unremittingly endorse.

Tell me something about him, I hear you saying. Very well. He's rather 'arty'; cultivates a taste for music, poetry, and things. Also interested in photography, and works in the X ray department at the hospital here. Like Wilbur, he conceals a desperate inferiority complex beneath flamboyant exhibitionism. He needs time to cool down — to mature as he is inclined to be impulsive, even obstreperous at times. Again like Wilbur, he has tried to aspire to the code of the empire-builder, and has been consistently ridiculed and squashed for his pains. It is this that has led to deep-seated feelings of inferiority resulting in indifference and tantrums. He swears volubly in public a lot as a means of letting off steam.

For the same reason he has a nasty habit of kicking at rough-looking dogs. The other afternoon whilst planting his boot on a couple of mangy specimens, the owner appeared and saw the deed. The man, an officer of sorts, was accompanied by some droopy female who kept bleating "Oh-how-could-you!" while Vere endured the flood of her husband's wrath. "I think you're the most loathesome object I've ever seen," he concluded, to which Vere responded with a sweet smile effectively closing the incident.

As I say, I believe this rather grotesque aspect of his personality is part of a transient phase, and there is no point in witholding his rightful place among us on account of it. I personally vouch for him unreservedly, as I am sure you will too when you have read his delicious, 'Dissertation on Eggs'.

Naturally we have trotted around Poona in tongas a good bit, and I have seen the inside of many a picture house and Chinese restaurant in his stimulating company. But our favourite haunt is the Forces Club, a building of much grandiloquence where on Sunday evenings amplified gramophone recitals of classical music are held. Last Sunday it was Mozart and Schubert; the week before, Rossini, Tchaikovsky, and Beethoven's 'Eroica'. I came away feeling like a watered flower! I had never heard the Eroica before. It's tremendous.

Wednesday

The results of the exam declared this morning. I repair to the Depot on Friday.

Damn this infernal pen!

March 9th 1946

Courney old lad,

Briefly, I'm back in Poona on leave. To fill in the story; I duly returned to my old home town for the fourth time to the usual joyous reception. Once again I was spotted in the offices by my buddy the Adjutant who began gesticulating wildly when he saw me. A tête-à-tête was quickly arranged for the following day.

Well, I had done a lot of hard thinking and was well-prepared for this interview. In the first place, I had decided that it was high time I had a spot of leave, not having had any since sailing from England's shores. When I had left Vere on the previous Thursday, I had in fact promised to meet him at 7 p.m. the following Monday at a certain cinema where the film version of Shaw's 'Pygmalion', starring Leslie Howard, was due to be shown. For my intention was to spend my leave loafing around Poona in Vere's estimable

101

company. I had expected fourteen days: in the event, the Adj. granted me one month without a moment's hesitation. He told me in despairing tones that I am his only professional failure. During a long career in India, he has contrived to fit every soldier in the medical corps into a steady job except myself. Well, I told him I thought I was cracking up under the strain of it all, and thinking this was the psychological moment to bare my anguished soul, so to speak, I did so. I used some pretty vivid language: actually said I felt like a bird imprisoned in a coal mine trying to get out, but judiciously refrained from making pathetic flapping movements with my hands — though I was tempted! I am to see him again when my leave is over, and I am quite certain he will do the best he can for me.

This interview took place on the Sunday, and the next day, having obtained the required papers, I was on my way back to Poona by an afternoon train. I went straight to the cinema, and when Vere arrived I was waiting for him. All he said was that he had to go to the lavatory urgently. . . "Where the _______ is it?" I pointed. "That?" he said, gazing stupidly at the ornate frontage. "Are you sure? I thought it was a Hindu shrine." As for 'Pygmalion'; it's simply superb, though I would have enjoyed almost anything that night. Vere thought it was splendid too.

I am staying at the Willingdon Club where I have a private room. It's a restful spot: a nice lounge, dance hall, swimming pool, billiards, etc., if you want that sort of thing. Personally, I don't. I just read, write, and loaf during the day; then in the evening when it gets cooler, I go somewhere or other with Vere. Usually it's a Chinese restaurant, then perhaps a movie and on to the Forces Club. Last night I tried eating my first (and last) Chop Suey. It can best be described as a volcano of shrimps, cat's tails, and bits of string erupting out of an omelette. I had to cancel the rest of the order!

Vere is excellent company, and puts up an impressive show in book shops, curio shops, and suchlike places. He has a fondness for bric-à-brac, old bronze, bits of carved soap-stone and the like. Or course India is teeming with hand-made stuff of this ilk. I don't think I've ever seen him buy anything except books, though; usually slender volumes of poetry. He liked Eliot and Louis MacNeice. But as I say, he puts up a great show just poking around these intriguing places. He picks something up and croons over it, like a child with a new toy. We both agree that Indian art is more properly described as a craft; pretty worthless unless seen in bulk.

I have hired a typewriter, and am typing out my essay which crystallizes my views on individualism, the army, and much else besides. It may come in useful when I next go before the Adjutant. Naturally, I shall be sending you a copy.


*March 15th 1946*

This morning my redoubtable bearer excelled himself. Along with the matutinal tea cup he brought me a letter from you. A somewhat depressing letter, I venture to add, in which you dismiss my newest cartoons with a terse criticism that might have been written by Humphrey Bogart or any other hard-boiled American. (I mention Bogart because I happened to see one of his films a few nights ago. . . "Hullo. Operator, the party doesn't reply. Get me police headquarters." He slips a king-sized cigarette between his lips, and has produced a gleaming lighter when a metallic voice barks from the other end of the line. "Hullo, is that police h.q.? Get me the Homicide Bureau. . .").

Now, I am not suggesting, old lad, that you have changed overnight into another Bogart; however, judging from your remarks, a little of this soulless brand of American vinegar seems to be seeping into your veins from somewhere. I concede that we had agreed to produce a commercial commodity, but I thought I had made my viewpoint clear: we were to evolve a style that was both saleable *and* original. So your assertion that I am "looking skyward" is right in the sense that I wish to avoid the usual

103

run-of-the-mill style of cartooning which, to my mind, is like shorthand drawing. . . For the present, let's shelve the subject.

My hopes for a quiet uneventful leave have received a rude jolt these past few days. Last Sunday morning a party of inebriated soldiers invaded the club and had to be rounded up by a detachment of red-caps; and a couple of nights ago I had a bit of an adventure on dance night. The place usually goes wild on these occasions; there's a lot of boozing and roistering, and I keep well out of the way. At eleven-thirty p.m. all was in full swing, and having shelved the idea of going to bed until things had quietened down a bit, I happened to spot a wart-hog staggering into his bunk along the corridor carrying the limp figure of a girl. With inflammatory visions of murder, rape, etc. clouding my mind, I crept down the passage to investigate. As I had guessed, the bloke was very drunk. In a few whisky-soaked words he told me the girl had passed out due to over-indulgence, and as he had no idea who she was, (she was Anglo-Indian and could not have been a day over sixteen) his chief concern was how to dispose of the body. Looking back on it, it strikes me that I may have interrupted a more sinister machination. As it was, I helped him carry the girl off the premises, and calling upon my skill as a medical orderly, brought her out of her coma. I poured cold water on the hapless child, in point of fact.

Where you have thousands of young men without any women in a tropical climate and in a foreign country where, in a sense, everyone is anonymous, strange deviant things are bound to happen; and once again, it is really the system that is to blame. My own attitude to sex is too negative for it to cause me much bother: I see it as a bestial — even a demonic impediment to mental quiescence.


*Thursday, March 21st 1946*

Well, this restorative sojourn is almost over, and I repair to the Depot on Saturday. No more surprises to report. I finished typing out my opus; a meritorious achievement which has left me quite enervated and a prey to the heat which appears to be upon us once again. More nervous symptoms: it's obvious I must get out of India fast.

Had a bit of difficulty persuading a Hindu shopkeeper to sell me one of his books the other day. (3 plays by Wilde) He didn't see me take it off the shelf, and thought I wanted to sell it to him! He knew no English; I know only a few Urdu phrases. So after five minutes futile altercation I decided an impasse had been reached and walked off taking the book with me. Well, I had sauntered a couple of furlongs or so when up comes the wallah gesticulating wildly, having discovered his error. Naturally I told him with well-feigned anger that the book was mine and that he was a raving imbecile, whereupon he bursts into tears and weeps unrestrainedly for several minutes till I finally relent and produce the money. It was only some time later that I discovered he had short-changed me! Such are the complications of shopping in an Indian bazaar.

I have been trying to coax Vere into reading Joad's 'Guide To Modern Thought' as he is so absurdly ignorant in some ways: he has no beliefs. But it is hopeless. He lives by impulse, and hasn't the reflective temperament. His chief impediment to meditation is a chronic inability to relax. I write these lines in the Forces Club, and he is scribbling a letter next to me now with such jittery abandon that one might think there was a time-bomb ticking away beneath his chair!

He now presides over the gramophone concerts, and selects the music himself. They have two turn-tables, you know, so there is only the slightest pause when the record comes to an end. And the amplifiers are up in the balcony so that the sound fills the air, just like an orchestra. All this music is new to me, and I listen with awe. Some of it (Haydn, for instance) is gay, elegant, even humorous. But what can you say about the Cesar Franck symphony? Rapturous. . . sublime. . . I unhesitatingly attest that these recitals have been a veritable ice-pack to the tortured Lewis soul.

I have seen some good movies too: 'Blithe Spirit' (a minor masterpiece); Olivier's 'Henry V' (a major masterpiece, I suppose; though I confess I am not a Shakespeare addict, and I stubbornly refuse to accept that every line he wrote is like a golden egg). But in particular, 'The Picture of Dorian Gray', which I have been assiduously watching for ever since your letter of five months ago. Never one for impetuous enthusiasms, I know that when you praise something as warmly as you did this film ("One of the very best pictures I have ever seen," you said) it is worth risking the price of a ticket. And my confidence was well-placed. George Sanders adorned with a Franz Hals beard looked amusing in the still photos outside the cinema, but the beard in motion as the actor declaimed Wilde's gems of cynicism was even more enchanting. The Army may have turned me into a cynic, old lad, but I'm not quite in the Lord Henry Wotton class yet!

P.S. Got stopped in the street by an Indian soothsayer this morning, and following a look at my palm and a mystical ritual involving rupee notes, he informed me I would leave India this year. Perhaps it's a good omen!

Sunday, March 31st 1946

Courtney old lad,

I must write you a few lines if only to keep my flagging spirits up! As you will see, I am back at the old hell-hole where there are no sympathetic souls. I am bored beyond endurance, and seem to be melting both physically and mentally: physically on account of the heat, and mentally on account of the hostile atmosphere (call it mental heat, if you like). At Deolali the wart-hog is at his insufferable worst. I spend most of my time in a sort of daze just wandering around trying to avoid them. But you can't in Deolali: they are too numerous.

Inevitably I have been put on guard duty. I woke up this morning and found I had spots on my stomach, and for the past three days I have been followed about by a bearded brute of a Sikh who obviously wants to start a beautiful friendship. Damn the Depot and all it stands for!

From the moment I got here everything seemed to go wrong; in fact the trouble began before I got here — the damn lorry broke down! This was a week ago. I was in pretty good spirits, rested and fresh from my month's leave, and determined to take it all in my stride. I sauntered into the old roost feeling like a homing pigeon. Even the char wallahs were beginning to look upon me as an old and valued customer.

Within hours the first blow fell. The Adjutant was on the point of leaving for England. A farewell binge was being held in his honour that very evening. And it was true. I watched from a place in the shadows as he addressed the convivial gathering. Of course there was only one thought in my mind: had he forgotten my case? Were all my efforts to be nullified? Would my future now depend on the tender mercies of a total stranger?

It was in a state of some anxiety that I presented myself before the new man the next morning, I can tell you. He seemed rather severe; quite different from my genial corpulent friend who had followed my chequered career from A to Z. Could I see him, I pleaded? For ten minutes I waited for the answer. . . Yes, I was to report to the office the following day.

Well, to cut the story short, old lad, I did see the Adj: it was a whirlwind interview lasting about three minutes in somebody else's office. "Well, Lewis," he said. "What are we to do with you? I could give you a job on the publicity staff at Delhi. How about that?" But I had made up my mind, and I didn't waver for an instant. I told him bluntly that I had had enough, that I had come to a dead end: could he get me discharged? "I can't personally discharge you from the service," he replied; "you understand that? But I have considered the psychiatric angle. I could write up a damn good case, if you want, and there would be no stigma attached."

Of course I accepted the offer gratefully, and there the matter rests. He has gone home now, so I am just hanging about here awaiting further developments. I have shot my bolt, old lad, and if his successors fail to follow the matter up, there is absolutely nothing I can do about it. Knowing the Army, I am not expecting to sail out of it without a hitch even if I get started. But if the worst comes to the worst and the whole scheme proves a total frost, I shall be none the worse off, shall I? Whatever the upshot, I can rest assured that I have done my very utmost to extricate this caterpillar from the inedible salad in which it finds itself.

Monday, All Fools Day

Another stab in the back! My name is on one of the drafts mustering in the Depot, and I can't convince the fool authorities that I shouldn't be on it. The thought of another field ambulance makes my blood run cold, as what thirst I ever had for the company of sweating, vituperating wart-hogs in the raw has long since been thoroughly assuaged. Typical Army bungling, of course. Didn't I say I expected something of the sort?

Am not going to post this till my fate is more certain.

April 7th 1946

I am still here, and breathing more freely. I am definitely off that draft, and I honestly believe that my name has been extricated from the posting machinery.

A missive from Vere yesterday containing his customary badinage has done much to raise my spirits. The Depot is totally devoid of his ilk. He writes that he managed to score three laughs the other night at the Forces Club while announcing Dvorak's New World Symphony. "I was then

109

pinioned to the wall by the piercing gaze of an Empire-builder. . ." Oh, if only I was back in Poona!

I have come to the conclusion that if I were stone deaf my life in the Army would have been comparatively painless. An academic point really, as in this case, I would never have been called up. What I mean is that it is the incessant cackling, swearing, the tramp of boots, the rattle of wagons and the blast of bugles that despoil the atmosphere. As I write a bugle is sounding, and hoards of believers hasten blindly to grovel in the dust in the scorching sun before that impeccably belted and booted idol — the pagan god Discipline. In control of these foolish hoards is the High Priest, the Sergeant Major. As for myself: as a self-confessed heretic I stand aside awaiting excommunication!

I am playing a game of hide-and-seek at present. During the day I contrive to blush unseen, a very difficult feat to achieve in this ant hill of madmen. Some parades, some duties are inescapable, and the occasional tiff with one of these little tin soldiers who live in a microscopic world of boots, gaiters, and cap badges is to be expected. In the evening I escape to the refuge of a cinema or to the Chinese restaurant where Wilbur and Desmond first met. The Chinese restaurant: the only flower in the Indian desert, Courtney. Egg fuyong is the one thing I shall miss when I leave India; that and perhaps also the illimitable supply of peanuts I habitually consume in the picture houses.

*April 15th*

Still living in a vacuum, waiting. How long can this go on? A minor event to report today. It seems I am wanted down at the hospital to draw a diagram or something for the Nose Specialist. At least it means the authorities haven't forgotten all about me.

*April 21st*

Easter Sunday. How well I remember the last one:

Wilbur and I attending the morning service in the lurching ship's lounge, and gamely rendering, 'For those in peril on the sea.' Happy days! Courtney. I attended no service today. I don't think marching along to a converted Nisson hut would be conducive to any sort of spiritual uplift.

April 26th

Have got five minutes to post this.

Laddie, it's happened! Have just been closeted with the psychiatrist. He wore no horn-rimmed spectacles, but even so he radiated understanding. After a month of nothing, things are moving at last. I am to report back to the hospital with my kit at once.

More later.

May 16th 1946

Courtney old lad,

Once more I put pen to paper as I know you must be wondering how things are progressing.

For the past two weeks or so I have been languishing here in the nut ward at the B.M.H., Bombay. On the board above my bed are inscribed the cryptic words, 'Psychopathic personality', and like the title of some ruthless gang of anarchists, the words strike trepidation and awe into the hearts of those who are curious enough to read them. You may picture me reclining here wearing a suitably enigmatic smile, and gently turning over the pages of a little book by H. G. Wells called, 'Mind At The End Of Its Tether'!

My fate is still uncertain, old lad, though I am content to stay here as long as they see fit as it is a very restful spot, the food is quite good, not the inedible pig swill I've been accustomed to, and I have got lots of books to read. The Maugham novel arrived yesterday: many thanks. Also a parcel of books (Mother's Christmas present!) reached me

111

while I was still at the Depot. So here I am with a bed on a covered veranda facing the road. In the leafy banyan trees opposite, comical jackdaws and huge swooping kite hawks disport themselves. Though I am quite free to move about, the Indian heat is not conducive to much exertion and I am content to sit on the veranda reading, writing, and perhaps doing a little sketching. As I say, a peaceful leisurely existence for a change, and I am thoroughly enjoying it!

At the back of my mind, of course, there lurks the anxious question, 'What next? Will there be a hitch?' But there is no sign that, behind the scenes, things are not proceeding smoothly. A week ago I went before a medical board (two Indian officers and the psychiatrist) but it was a very perfunctory affair and only lasted a couple of minutes. I was not questioned.

The psychiatrist had travelled up to Deolali to see me, for I was sent down here the next morning. And when they confined me in a padded cell for the night I honestly felt I had found my rightful niche at last! Yes, old lad, in a society of madmen the lunatic alone is sane! But seriously, it was a darling little padded cell with a barred window and a cute wrought-iron gate with spikes. Right down by the water's edge to minimize escape, I suppose. But the sea view was sublime and the air gorgeously fresh. You would have loved it! In fact, anyone who had been forced to sleep in barrack rooms for two years would have loved it. I am sure Wilbur loved it; for he must have been there. Perhaps my inner jubilance was visible, for the two orderlies who relieved me of my razor and bootlaces on my admission were beaming throughout the procedure.

I was kept there in the rabbit run for two nights along with three other inmates who, like myself, were quite docile. They seemed rather depressed, otherwise quite ordinary. Regrettably I was then removed from my sanctuary (no doubt to make way for some other poor soul whom the Army had driven bonkers) and directed to the open ward which has been my domicile ever since.

Broken souls, old lad! That's what this ward consists of:

the mutilated minds of pitiful misfits — the Army's handiwork. In the bed on my right is a rough, ugly, illiterate jail-bird: an ex-coal-miner, almost inarticulate, who says he has committed murder. Not, you may think, the ideal choice for a bed-side companion, yet I find I can talk to him for hours! He has imagination, or rather — incipient imagination, because having only seen the backside of the picture of life, his spirit has remained uncultivated. In the bed on my left there is a clean-cut, intelligent R.A.F. sergeant, but I have hardly exchanged a word with him so far because he seems utterly prosaic. I accompanied my mad murderer pal to some sort of Red Cross char and wad (tea and cake) get-together last Saturday where an incredibly boring time was had by all. I suppose it was intended to be therapeutic.

Of course I hadn't been here for a week before I ran into Eddie. Just as vague and disconsolate as ever, but good to talk to. I have been downtown, of course, and have dutifully paid my respects to the Gateway of India. Truly an empire-builder's edifice, although built to last. Bombay itself can best be described as an over-grown bazaar.

Bought some more books there including two by Beverly Nichols: 'Verdict on India' and 'Cry Havoc!'. Perhaps it is all carefully stage-managed, but he seems to me to lead an ideal existence; that of the wandering individualist romantically seeking the grail of beauty and knowledge! The contrast with my own peregrinations in the forces is so immense that I concede my judgement of Nichols' writing may not be detached. It also makes me aware of the utter worthlessness of my own travels as literary material; for obviously if one is pushed into a cattle truck bulging with wart-hogs, and constantly humiliated by N.C.O.s or M.P.s for not wearing a cap or some other equally trivial 'offence', one's observations and attitudes are bound to be warped and cynical. Trying to write literature as a private in the Army is, I should think, as futile as trying to play Beethoven piano sonatas in a busy NAAFI canteen.

'Cry Havoc!', I might say, is a defence of pacifism; and it is obvious to me now that I should have contrived to register as a conscientious objector myself back in 1943. But what could I do without guidance? They got me while I was such a shrimp!

But the two outstanding books I have just read are Aldous Huxley's 'Brave New World' and Bernard Shaw's 'Everybodys' Political Whats-What?'. The Huxley is a story about a utopian civilization of the future founded on the suppression of individualism. So you can see why it interested me: the result was a nightmare society very similar to the Army. Huxley's exposure of the soullessness of this system is superb, and I urge you to read the book if you have not already done so. As for the Shaw, it is a truly amazing *tour de force* for a man nearly ninety: his sagacity is that of an old man, yet he still writes like an *enfant terrible*. He begins by posing the question, 'Is human nature incurably depraved?' And his answer is basically 'no'; an answer which I regretfully decline to agree with. It has always been my contention that militarism and war come naturally to the overwhelming majority of men; how otherwise could wars be fought? I have proved from my own experience that one does not *have* to get caught up in it. Passive resistance to the war machine can and does result in one's rejection by it; from which it follows that if enough people put up sufficient resistance, the machine would grind to a halt. What I am saying is that when you see those long lines of battle-weary troops slogging through the mud in the news reels don't waste any sympathy on them: they only have themselves to blame for being there.

The truth is that they *want* to be there; they believe in what they are doing. If they did not, they would break down under the strain and horror of it all, like so many of the patients on this ward. I have studied them guardedly, and it seems to me that they have one thing in common which can best be called a streak of individualism. And, of course, it is only the individualist who is capable of non-conformity. It is not surprising that the fundamental principle underlying military discipline is the suppression of individualism, as it is through a few recalcitrant individuals alone that the danger of demoralization lies. This is also the theme underlying Huxley's fascist utopia: so one can draw the conclusion that it is only through the efforts of the individualist that mankind can be saved from annihilating itself in an orgy of destruction, or sinking into the sort of abysmal ant-heap described in 'Brave New World'. This is why I unremittingly oppose all doctrines and political parties which do not place freedom of the individual first and foremost. The one insuperable objection to Shaw's Soviet-style socialism is that within such a system, he himself would be among the first to be 'liquidated'. Having said this, I must confess I prefer the socialist Aneurin Bevan to that war-monger individualist Churchill. Bevan: the man who says he abhors "the Poona mentality".

Strolled along the sea wall at dusk this evening and gazed at the twinkling lights that surround the bay. A scene reminiscent of Disney. Yet seen close to they would all be smelly little lamps illuminating filthy stalls. . . A moral of some sort here, I think!

*May 20th 1946*

I have just been informed that I am to be invalided back to England. Hurrah! whoopee! and all the rest of it. Of course I cannot be sure till I get there that I shall be released altogether, but if I can't manage this final hurdle having cleared so many, I'm a Dutchman! Feel a great sense of relief.

*June 3rd*

Well, old lad, I regret to announce that the picture has changed since my last bulletin and I seem to be tottering on the verge of a nervous breakdown. I spent the whole night walking round the huge ward in a state of near panic, and this morning am utterly exhausted. More later — I hope.

*June 5th*

Seem to have rcovered my equilibrium for the nonce, but am inwardly shaken. My friend, the jail-bird, who went

away this morning told me he also suffers from this ailment
— acute anxiety, though I had not noticed any symptoms.
They had brought in a dying man that afternoon which
might have something to do with it. A suicide, poisoned: the
stomach pump kept sucking away half the night till the poor
bloke expired. When I picturesquely told the psychiatrist
that my nerves were as taught as a violin string it was
nothing less than the truth. I can honestly say that I have
always fought clean with the Army and cannot be accused of
falsifying my case with a view to 'working my ticket'.

Can't explain these things: my nerves are just shot,
that's all. Yet this evening I was laughing heartily at an
ENSA revue, seemingly none the worse for the trauma. I've
not reported the incident as they might take me off the
repatriation list for treatment. I am due to go back to Deolali
next week — so I've heard — for 'documentation'. So will
write you again from there.


June 17th 1946

Courtney old lad,

Am at the Homeward Bound Trooping Depot. What a
place. Set somewhere in the Deolali desert, the camp
abounds with wart-hogs, dead dogs, and great big black
vultures. Seem to have caught some sort of skin disease off
their filthy lavatories and have had my private parts painted
purple! Trust Deolali; it's always good for a laugh.

I nearly died a couple of days ago, old lad. Yes, I
thought I had penned you my last missive. Severe nerve
attack: not exactly foaming at the mouth, but so distraught
that I staggered straight to the little hospital where an
amiable Indian doctor administered a knock-out drop that
put me out like a light. I woke up the next morning after
umpteen hours sleep feeling utterly exhausted; scarcely able
to move. Nobody told me anything, so I just lay there trying
to decide whether I had had a nervous breakdown or a heart

116

attack. As everyone in the bloody place was laughing at me, I concluded it was not the latter. Their attention seemed confined to a case of suspected rabies.

My diagnosis confirmed today as I have been discharged from the place. Feel much steadier after lots of sleep, but still very shaky. It seems we join the ship tomorrow. Even twenty-four hours ago I would have ruled this out as a physical impossibility, but now I am determined to be on it. I have run a long race, and I am damn well not going to fall at the last fence with the winning post in sight! Somehow I am going to get up that gangway, and if I collapse on the deck it doesn't matter: the ship will take me home even if I spend the voyage in the sick bay.

One of the fellows on this draft has charge of our papers, and I have managed to get a look at the medical report on my case: 'A misfit since his schooldays. . . he is a caricature of a soldier. . . Obsessed with his little drawings. . . cannot tolerate a communal life. . . A tall clean youth in the depths of despair.'

Well, Courtney, the Adj. said he could write up a damn good case for me and he has done so. I am sure you will agree when I describe these observations as gems of truth. The sad thing is that each one of them was just as true two years ago — the length of time it has taken me to rub them in. Ah, well! I'm not complaining. I convinced the authorities in the end.

On all sides the wart-hogs are cramming the most incredible rubbish into large suitcases, piles of cheap Indian bric-à-brac to take home as presents. Needless to say, I have not bought so much as an ivory toothpick; indeed, one toothpick more in addition to the young library of books crammed into my pack and I might not get up that gangway! The orders are that no man may board ship with more than he can carry himself.

Those who aren't busy packing are sitting around discussing football and greyhound racing. One would never guess they were on the eve of repatriation: there is no excitement at all. It bears out my contention that they feel as much as home in the Army as they do out of it. I even get the impression that some of them are rather sad at the prospect of demob!

Well, old lad, must close. Must get a good sleep before the final hop.

P.S. Have just seen a simply fantastic sunset: iridescent gold splashed across vivid cobalt traversed by a glorious rainbow. The whole sky was a blaze of colour. Let's hope it is the last I shall see in this inimical land.

Aboard that worthy vessel, the S.S. Cameronia<br>June 23rd 1946

Courtney old lad,

I don't know if this will be readable: I am scribbling it on the back of an old copy of Oliver Twist on A Deck of the above-mentioned garbage scow. I am aware that you have never been so fortunate as to take a health cruise on a troop ship, but in case you are ever tempted to do so, let me tell you it is largely a case of bathing in a leaky cupful of salt water, and living in a perpetual queue of sweating wart-hogs, most of whom are covered in ringworm. And in case you think I exaggerate, let me tell you that I got my first chance of getting a wash my fourth day on board. The heat on that mess deck is like an oven, and believe me I needed it. Not that I am prone to worry myself about such mundane trivialities; but what with the heat, constipation, another head cold and a bad attack of *mal de mer* the first day at sea, I confess to feeling a little bit sorry for myself (as usual, I suppose).

But laddie, it's the end! I know I ought to be throwing my hat in the air on gaining a berth (ha! ha!) on this old tub (a priviledge thousands of home-sick soldiers would doubt-less give a year's cigarette ration for), but I'm bound to say I survey the outcome of this voyage with some trepidation. Yes, Courtney, your old pal Graham is at present a prey to sickness and despondency. I am willing to bet you would

118

have constipation too if you saw the long line of bowls in the A Deck lav. I daren't go near it before 1 a.m.!

Ran into some bloke who had come out on the Strathmore with me and Wilbur. When he said I have changed considerably I emitted a hollow laugh.

Apart from all my other worries, the blasted boat seems to be going *backwards* at the moment!

You once mentioned that if you have learnt anything in the forces it is that the chasm between yourself and your fellow men is wide. In my case it is unbridgeable. Why, oh why, for instance, when one's nerves are stretched to breaking point does somebody want to start playing the banjo? I tell you, old lad, five days out and I've had my fill of this shipful of guffawing, sun-bronzed, medallioned and bush-hatted wart-hogs! I was five minutes late for dinner today, and arrived to find the pigs had eaten my share. I just gave them a contemptuous look and buzzed off. I am playing a mysterious taciturn role on this voyage, largely because I want to conserve my nervous energy.

The sea air seems to have improved my nerves in some mysterious way. I am resting as much as I can, and am glad to say I have had no more seizures like the one I described in my last. A nasty turn, old lad. Of course I know it is all in my mind: anyone as highly-strung and imaginative as I am is vulnerable to hysteria and hallucinations when subjected to a prolonged period of stress. In the past I have seriously believed myself to be developing the symptoms of all sorts of incurable diseases. But I always pull out of it, and I expect my eventual demise will be due to a loose chimney pot or carelessly aimed golf ball! In the present instance, I am confident a few months rest in congenial surroundings will restore me to health.

There are people who may say that my tribulations have been nothing compared to the terrors endured by a front-line soldier, but I don't have to tell you that, to a sensitive person, spiritual torments can be as severe as a good measure of physical suffering. The wart-hog's two great advantages are, first, his gregariousness, and second, his unquestioning belief in what he is doing. You can't make a soldier of a man who has neither of these qualities.

Am quite absorbed in 'Oliver Twist'. It strikes me his tribulations somewhat resemble my own. Dickens, like Wodehouse, is a great literary caricaturist; and like P.G., he is one of those elite authors who have created a world apart.

Wednesday, July 2nd or 3rd 1946
(Not sure which: Time plays tricks on board ship.)

I am now in the Mediterranean, and no disasters to report. Yesterday the O.C. Troops — a consummate empire-builder if ever I heard one wheeze down the inter-com — briefly announced that we were not to be surprised if the ship hit a mine as a school of stray ones were reported to be drifting down from the Adriatic. But it seems to be a false alarm as the ship steams merrily onward.

Things are looking up, old lad. Despite everything, I feel much stronger and steadier since I began this missive. I am smoking a lot and reading a lot (Shaw's 'Plays Unpleasant'), and avoiding conversation as much as I can. The weather is perfect, and the sea hypnotic: I allow it to soothe me into a comatose lethargy. I feel I have had my turn in the ring, and it is gratifying just to lean back and let the Army do something for me; (*for* me and not *to* me, for a change!)

Saw a film show sitting on the deck in the moonlight the other eve; the sea like a mill pond. (Edward G. in 'Double Indemnity'. Good.) During the show the Empress of India steamed past looking like a fairy palace, and gave us a hoot.

(Later)

What a surprise! Have just attended a lecture in one of the ship's lounges. The place was packed out to hear an eminent painter, Augustine Booth, expounding the subject of fine art. A distinguished figure with a grey beard, he seems to have broken an arm which was resting in a sling made from a brightly coloured bandana. His theme: that Art is the

120

expression of emotion, and not necessarily of beauty. True
Art, in fact, can be ugly, though he does not consider all
forms of expressionism to be true Art. Surrealism is not true
Art because it is meaningless. Not, you might think, very
promising stuff to give the troops. Yet he held his audience
which he handled with great cunning, I thought. As for
myself, I have come away refreshed from this brief sniff of
rarefied ozone from another world. An extended course of
this treatment will put me right, I am sure.

So I came out on deck to find a sunset that would
doubtless send Mr Booth rushing off to find his paints, if he
were able to handle a brush. There had been some beautiful
sunsets and sunrises in the Red Sea, but this one silhouetting
the black outline of Cape Bon was the most beautiful of all. I
was so carried away as to blurt out something ecstatic to a
strange wart-hog nearby. He was leaning over the gunwale
smoking, and I don't think he had noticed the sky. He looked
up for a moment, and then replied: "How high d'you think
that island is, mate?" At which point the brief conversation
closed.


*Sunday, July 7th*

Made a dutiful pilgrimage to the church service this
morning, and delivered thanks to God for watching over my
fortune. I've had a lot of luck finding my way out of this
swamp, and I seem to detect the hand of Providence. Call
this superstitious moonshine, if you like.

We passed Gibraltar yesterday and are now steaming
across a quiescent Biscay. I didn't see the rock, not being one
of the stalwarts prepared to get up and peer into the darkness
at 4 a.m. Unless the propeller drops off or something, we
should reach Britain (I hesitate to say Blighty!) in three
days.

*July 10th*

When an escort of cheerful healthy-looking sea-gulls
met the ship yesterday I knew we were home. What a
contrast to the cunning Indian kite-hawk! This morning I

awoke to find the ship at anchor; and on either side of us, an adorable Clydeside scene whose sombre quaintness surpasses all the harsh grandeur that India has to offer. There is only one word to describe that grass out there — verdant!

Well, old lad, that's it. I will post this as soon as I get ashore, and then send you a wire when I reach home.

July 24th 1946

Courtney old lad,

I am comfortably ensconced in my own room, a case full of my favourite books beside me, and a Cheshire cat made of green pottery beaming down at me from the window ledge. The window is festooned with ivy, and the last clouds of a dull morning are hurrying away behind a cluster of robust green trees and sturdy chimney pots over the way.

My apologies for waxing so lyrical, old lad, but after such a long spell in the Indian desert, it bathes the Lewis wounds to languish in the delights of Broad Leas and the surrounding English loveliness. My first day home, after donning my Scottish tweeds and the old American ox-bloods (and, of course, after sending you a triumphant cable) I wanted nothing more than to take the dog for a walk and inhale the resuscitating English ozone exuded by the healthy trees, fine hedges and other green foliage. Even the cows look cleaner than the average Indian. Wending my way to a little music shop, I then purchased recordings of the Nut Cracker Suite to return home in time for tea when I heard some cheery empire-builder on the radio describe the applause at Lords as "the finest music known to Man." And I'm not being cynical, old lad; really I'm not!

As my wire informed you, I arrived home on the 11th by an early milk train from Chester. A quaint little engine it was, that puffed and whistled in the sparkling sunshine. It might have been copied from a drawing by Emett. Of course I had sent Mother a wire from Scotland, and she knew I was

122

coming. She is very well, and — as I say — everything is delightful: everything, that is, except the Gateway of India, and that will have to go! This is a colossal Queen Anne cupboard affair which takes up most of the dining-room, and which resembles the monstrous edifice on view at Bombay. It is a far harder thing to squeeze through the eye of a needle than it is to squeeze into our dining-room furnished with the Gateway of India. (?)

But I'm weak, old lad, infernally weak. I seem to have next to no power of concentration. I just wallow sumptuously in the atmosphere and take Brock the cairn terrier for the occasional trot. The fact is I only just made it in time to avert a mental breakdown of disturbing dimensions. I get these seizures when I feel like a harp string that has just been twanged! My heart does a Cossack dance, and I collapse in an inanimate heap. I had one at lunch time the other day, and Mother frantically phoned the doctor who arrived with his mouth full of Yorkshire pudding, and diagnosed me a nervous wreck. He also said I was extremely introspective. I suppose it is all a big reaction: after weeks of biting the bullet I have just let myself go. Yet my leave is up in two weeks; in fact I have just been notified to report to some booby-hatch in Scotland on August 7th. How I'm going to manage, the Lord only knows.

*Sunday, August 4th 1946*

Far too much has been happening. Yesterday Wilbur left for London after a week's stay! On his way he had to keep a lunch engagement in Liverpool I had made with my father: I was too exhausted to go. Also, Peter came in last week-end wearing square-rig and bursting with youthful exuberance which made me feel like a wizened sage. He has some thoroughbred English filly in tow.

But to revert to Wilbur. He phoned me from Brixton jail (London) where he has been incarcerated following some unfortunate car smash while he was running an illicit taxi service. The next day he arrived with only the clothes he stood up in due to the fact that his belongings had been confiscated for failing to pay his hotel bill. What an imbroglio!

Anyway, we had an enjoyable week padding around Liverpool and places buying gramophone records and things. We have made a celebration gramophone record! Two records, to be precise, as Wilbur did one solo having written some lyrics to Dvorak's Humoresque. It goes like this:

Think of days back in Deolali,
Land of politician's folly,
Wooden charpoys, wogs, and adjutants.
Then along to blighted Poona
In a wart-hog's prairie schooner:
Fatigues and stiff starched pants. . .

(You have to pronounce 'fatigues' — 'fat-i-gez', or it doesn't rhyme!)

Wilbur is toiling for some wine magnate in London at present, but this is only a stop-gap occupation until he discovers his true vocation. He does not consider himself cut out to be a wage slave. He is thinking of going to Switzerland, and I might accompany him.

I have also received a long letter from Desmond who is languishing quite happily in Ceylon following a helpful interview with a psychiatrist which Wilbur obtained for him last year. I had never heard about this. His intellect seems to be on the boil as he says he has written a play. He is now planning a trip on the Norfolk Broads when his shackles are finally loosed. So I amend my previous enjoinment to watch out for a suitable caravan: for 'caravan' now read 'motor boat'!

I expect you heard about Shaw's ninetieth birthday. An auspicious occasion, old lad. I heard him make an impromptu speech on the radio. It was also televized. Must confess to being deeply moved. How different his voice sounds from the idiot barkings of sergeant-majors and the pompous nasal noises emitted by aloof empire-builders! He is a living inspiration, and I feel I owe him a personal debt for helping to keep me sane during my recent trials.

Talking of sergeant-majors: I am seriously thinking of changing my surname by deed-poll as almost every R.S.M. of belligerent aspect I ever met was named Lewis! I maintain that everyone should have the right to choose a name to his personal liking in the same way as he selects his own particular brand of tobacco. Don't you agree?

All for the present, Will write from Scotland.

P.S. Have not heard from you since March.

Friday, August 9th 1946

Courney old lad,

Have decided to make this letter a series of short entries.

The loony-bin is a civilian retreat in the Scottish glens a few miles from Glasgow, which I reached on Tuesday assisted by a bottle of brandy and my Uncle Geoff. By a stroke of luck he had to come up here on business, so I travelled with him.

The presiding Psych is the same bird I saw when I disembarked a month ago; an inscrutable Scot with the customary forbidding horn-rimmed spectacles. Yesterday's interview did not go so well, and I did not sleep much last night being a prey to a veritable turmoil of doubts and worries. I gave him a copy of the Poona essay, and am now thinking this was a mistake.

Saturday, August 10th

Crisis over! The Doctor took off his spectacles this morning disclosing a human being and not the Freudian bogey-man I had feared. It seems that my essay is the psychiatrist's dream! He is writing a book on psychopaths, and so now he's got lots of data straight from the horse's mouth. He was quite effulgent about it. Did I know I was classed with violent criminals of the worst type? he remarked impassively. My self-confidence was returning rapidly. Apparently, 'psychopath' is a blanket term covering all

125

types of loners and wild men. I have even read somewhere that, had they lived today, Leonardo da Vinci and Lawrence of Arabia would be put in this category. He went on to say that the Army was no place for me, and that I would be out of it in three weeks. There was just one proviso: he would like to see Mother, and wanted to know if she could come up here? I said if it was necessary I am sure she would do so, and I wrote her about it this evening.

Friday, August 16th

The Psych told me off the record that the patients in this booby-hatch have one thing in common: one way or another, they are inadequate people and cannot cope with life. They are a harmless crowd of lost souls really, though with very negative personalities, and consequently impossible to talk to except at a superficial level.

Of course, they are creating a bit of noise this evening just when I want to listen to the tribute to H. G. Wells on the radio. He died on Wednesday. (Later) Managed to hear it despite local interference: a dramatization of his story, 'The Kingdom of the Blind', a parable elucidating the isolation of the sage in an ignorant world. Profound indeed.

Sunday, August 18th

Once again my nerves are curling at the ends (to quote Wodehouse). All this hanging about in this dreary place has got me down. Yesterday I sent for Wilbur in desperation. I procured some dope from the Doctor who calls my ailment 'hysteria', but what calms me more than anything is watching the old men playing bowls. I defy anyone to throw a fit while watching this game which is strictly for somnambulists. There was a blackbird on one end of the green this afternoon, and I watched it enviously as it hopped about pecking for worms. Many is the time I have envied the freedom of birds and animals living in a natural state free from the man-made mesh of civilization with its insufferable armies, navies, factories, and constant hustle and bustle, wear and tear.

126

But why am I so depressed? I should be rejoicing in the knowledge that I am poised on the threshold of escape from this mesh. Yet I am not; most decidedly, I am not.

The weather is dismal and cold; not at all summery.

Saturday, August 24th

For the first time since I arrived here I have lost that dreadful feeling of walking about on stilts and in imminent peril of falling in a heap at any moment. In short, I feel relaxed and — dare I say it? — happy. The reason, of course, is that Mother arrived in Glasgow last night, and this afternoon came to the hospital where she spent thirty minutes in the Doctor's inner sanctum. Afterwards we went for a stroll before she departed for her hotel, happy in the knowledge that I shall be returning home before another week has passed.

There are formalities, of course, in the form of a medical board, and some long train journeys; but with my goal in sight I know I shall find the will-power to overcome these obstacles. If I could survive that interminable sea voyage, I'm damned sure I can stagger through the demob process.

Thursday, August 29th

I'm out, old lad, a free man!

I am writing this on the puff-puff steaming south. The medical board transpired yesterday: as I said, a formality. The withering eye of the presiding e.b. wilted into the semblance of a mere poached egg under the Doctor's inscrutable gaze. You know, during one of my sessions with him I actually remarked on the unnerving effect of his horn-rimmed spectacles!

With two fellow psychopaths I entrained at once for the smithy at York where the chains were finally severed. And now, as I say, I am on my way to a new life dressed in an ill-fitting brown suit and matching felt hat.

Too tired to marshal my thoughts, old lad. Will post this when I get to Liverpool.

127

Courtney old lad,

The gentle morning sunshine is streaming through the ivy-adorned window of the little study, and is illuminating the soap stone carving of the two quaint Chinamen I have placed on the bookcase. It is also illuminating two letters from you which came this morning. One is dated May 20th and has pursued me round the globe; the other August 15th. Their arrival has elated me considerably. I regret that you failed to send such missives during my lonely vigils on mountain tops, in deserts, and in the various nut wards I have frequented when I was prey to the dark chasms of despondency. However, old lad, let's forget it. It's all over and done with now, and your apology is warmly accepted.

As one of your remarks suggests that you may have misconstrued the point, I would like to reassure you that my health is sound organically. Since my return from Lennoxtown I have been taking things very easy, and my nervous system is much more stable. It goes to show that the seat of my recent afflictions was purely psychological: they were signals from my embattled mind to say that it had had enough. You realize, old lad, that from start to finish the forces ranged against me were out to destroy my integrity — that is, everything I instinctively stand for.

Of course, I dissembled my nervous condition as much as I could for fear of being held for treatment, and there were one or two anxious moments as I have frankly told you. For close on two days when I was in Scotland my heart was beating out a rhythm like a South American samba. But I'd had this before at Deolali, and having learnt it was not fatal, I just got hold of some dope and sat it out.

So the process went ahead unimpeded, and I was duly given an honourable discharge as an incorrigible misfit — the squarest of pegs in the roundest of holes. To quote a line from the official papers on my case, I was deemed to be 'a waste of the Army's time and the King's money.' And I could not have put it better myself!

In your other letter you say, "I believe I'd go stark mad if I had to spend eighteen more months in the service." Well, old lad, I nearly did, and I know how you must feel. The treatment for this frame of mind is, of course, some solicitude from the boys in the horn-rimmed specs, as I do assure you, in case you are assailed by doubts, that you are a perfect specimen of a 'psychopath' and in consequence a waste of the President's time and money. You should demand your inalienable right to an honourable discharge without a minute's delay!

But a word of warning from one who has trod the path. Although a short cut, strait is the gate and rocky is the way; and while many do start, few are chosen. Preliminary spade-work is necessary to show that you are unadaptable, by which I mean you have to have a record. So I suppose my considered advice would be this: adapt if you possibly can without becoming irreversibly changed or mentally affected. I found this impossible myself, but at a pinch, you appear to have found it is not. Only make a break for the psychiatrist's back door when it becomes imperative to seek an emergency exit. In either case, I trust it will not be long before the ghastly interlude is over for you as it is for me. And when it is, remember, you are welcome here for a protracted sojourn whenever you wish to come. Just send me a wire when the great day approaches, "Sailing S.S. Bath Tub such-and-such a date", and you can depend on the warmest of welcomes. The food situation is not as bad as it is painted.

For myself, a long period of well-earned rest and recuperation seems to be indicated; in fact, I have done enough travelling to last me for the next five years at least.

Yesterday I received a communication from a captain on the staff of a certain Scottish military hospital. Enclosed was a chit which I had previously returned due to the omission of an all-important rubber stamp mark, and on it were inscribed the words, 'Any inconvenience caused to you is regretted.' The chit was my discharge form; and believe me, laddie, there is a story behind those words of which you more than anyone know the details! I have waited a long

long time to hear the Army apologize.

I have started a collection of orchestral records, and judging from your own list of favourites, our taste in music seems to correspond. Tried any Rossini overtures yet? As I write, the effervescent sound of his 'Italian Girl in Algiers' is coming over the radio. It is infused with his usual gaiety and wit: I can hear that mischievous piccolo darting about all over the place making fools of the double basses! Yesterday Mother and I attended Mozart's 'Marriage of Figaro' in Liverpool. It turned out to be musical Wodehouse.

P.G.'s latest novel, 'Money in the Bank', has just been published. One of the books he wrote while a prisoner, it is understandably not his best though palatable. I will send you a copy for Christmas.

Thanks again for your sententious letters, old lad.

P.S. Wilbur is thinking of visiting America.

*September 19th 1946*

Courtney old lad,

Your letter came this morning. You say, "If Wilbur knows what's good for him he won't spend much time in the U.S." In point of fact, it now seems doubtful that he will be spending any time in the U.S. Things have been happening, and it looks as if he's going on the stage! You will recall that he was working for a wine merchant? Well, he has never made any attempt to conceal the incontrovertible fact that he is unsuited for the conventional desk job, and it was not very long before his employer also made this discovery whereupon he once more found himself looking for work. But as you are aware, no sooner is Wilbur tossed into the boiling surf, so to speak, than he rises upon the crest of an oncoming wave. And this time he seems to have landed the leading role in some play being performed by an amateur dramatic club. So now, elated at the thought of playing dashing young heroes, he has resolved to pass some sort of test enabling him to obtain a place at the Royal Academy of Dramatic Art.

You can see that unless this new wave of fortune suddenly subsides plunging him back into the boiling surf, he will not be visiting America until such time as he is required to appear on Broadway or somewhere. I personally think that he is singularly well cut out for the stage: he is a hell of an exhibitionist, completely self-possessed and speaks clearly. Perhaps a bit on the short side, he is reasonably good-looking, though I regret he has shaved off the moustache he sported whilst in the Army which gave him an engaging devil-may-care look.

So much for Wilbur — at least for the moment. Oh, I should mention that he sent me some ideas for cartoons which he thinks he can sell for me! They all satirize the British empire-builder in a gleeful sort of way. I have done the work and did not make my previous mistake of being too subtle, having learnt that there is no market for subtle cartoons.

I also received a letter from Desmond a few days ago in which he said, "I shall soon be following in yours and Wilbur's footsteps. . ." It appears he has been placed on a charge which he considers unjust, and he is going to dig in his heels and refuse all punishment in the hope that he will eventually end up in the psychiatrist's sanctum.

Vere also seems to be going through the mangle. He has just got over an attack of pleurisy and complains about numerous tiffs he has been having with the hospital authorities. All this against the background of the current Poona riots. (Two primitive hoards of brown pock-marked wart-hogs crossing kukris!) I commiserate with him.

*September 21st*

I woke up this morning to find the bedroom swimming round in circles and my mouth like a mustard plaster. I had been dreaming of empire-builders with thick bristly moustaches, so you see my nerves are far from right yet.

A momentous letter from Desmond. "I was given 7 days c.b. Refused it. 14 days. Refused. 21 days. Refused. Attended a Summary of Evidence as a preliminary to a Court Martial which is coming off later this year. Naturally I've got them all guessing. . . When I am asked for my defence, I shall say in a suitably vacant tone, 'There is no defence. I have nothing to say. The whole thing is stupid.' If I maintain that attitude they can do only one thing — send me before the psychiatrist."

Your prayers are requested, old lad, and your encouragement. You can supply the latter by writing to the old boy at the address below.

Wilbur had lunch with Desmond's twenty-three year-old sister the other day, and did his best to reassure her. As I said in my last, he has been acting as my agent in Fleet Street of late, and the cartoons are now in the offices of 'Punch'. They have been turned down by the editor of another leading magazine who has taken the trouble to express his opinions in a letter. He writes: "*You* know what is lying behind the pictures but it would not be clear to our readers, and I think the drawings themselves are a little confused. I don't mean I want an absolutely classical line, but I think you go too far in the opposite direction and turn out drawings which are more bewildering than funny."

What he calls a little confused and bewildering is of course my masterly distortion! Anything original is bound to be looked at askance at first, and I am fully aware that the ice will take a little cracking. However, I could not hope for a better agent than Wilbur.

Well, old lad, I must close as I can sniff the supper — meat-roll containing the following: two units worth of bread, half the day's milk ration, a slice of bacon, and a dried egg! Such is life in battle-torn Britain.

P.S. You might like to know that I haven't had a haircut since I was up in Scotland, and indeed have made a vow never to go to a barber's shop again.

Courtney old lad,

Thanks for your letter and, especially, for the photo. You look as sardonic as ever. I also gratefully acknowledge receipt of two books; more about which in a moment.

But to begin with: Wilbur has just paid me a surprise two-day visit, this time accompanied by Desmond's sister Monica. She must be an intrepid girl to have decided, at a moment's notice, to entrust the wheel of her Hillman Minx to the notorious Wilburforce in an endeavour to reach the Lewis mansion, using all her saved up petrol coupons in the process. They arrived with only a couple of pounds between them on Wednesday night, and Wilbur had to enlist the help of the local police to obtain rooms at such a late hour. They set off south again this morning in a thick fog, and have probably got hopelessly lost by now as the fog is said to be enveloping the whole of the country.

Desmond's sister resembles him both facially and temperamentally: she shares his phlegmatic calm. She works for the B.B.C. and met Wilbur after he had got in touch with her about Desmond. She saw his great stage debut which seems to have been acclaimed a success, though Wilbur himself is rather sober about it all and told me he had 'met his Waterloo.' Of course, one has to remember that he has no more training for the stage than I have for Art, and the mere fact that he took on the leading role in this show is a feat whether he pulled it off or not. He told me beforehand he thought he could do so "with sufficient grimaces and gesticulations" but no one, least of all Wilbur, would pretend that this amounts to stage technique.

By the way, I am currently engaged in illustrating an extremely funny piece written by Wilbur at an editor's suggestion called, 'An Englishman Buys A Car'. Naturally I shall send you a print of this, or any other specimen of my published work as soon as I receive it. Wilbur is to get 50% of my takings at the moment, for, as he judiciously points out: (a) it is he who will have found the market, and (b) he needs the money desperately! But if he gets any drawings into the Strand magazine (and he thinks there is a strong possibility), he will have earned every penny of his whack in my opinion.

Now, about bringing over this Virginia ham. . . I applaud this brainwave, in fact the ham Must Come First when, in the not too distant future, you pack your suitcase, hand grip, or whatever you do pack. If it means leaving a pair of socks behind (or Volume 5 of your 'Life of Robert E. Lee') don't hesitate to do so, Courtney, because — as I say, the Ham has pride of place. The last time I so much as smelt a ham, and this was no superior Virginian specimen, was towards the end of 1943 when I visited my now defunct Aunt Minnie; and where she obtained it, I wouldn't like to say! For the past two years I have been living with a more or less permanent tummy upset, though I hasten to add that since I first staggered off that troop ship, I have put on 6 pounds in weight. I am hoping that by the time you get here, my digestive processes will have recovered sufficiently to enable me to tackle a ham with relish.

Despite diminutive rations I am feeding far better now than I ever did on Army grub. Of course we have our own hens. But the bacon ration has just been reduced to one slice a week. Other items per week are: 2 pints of milk; 4 ozs of butter; 2 ozs of margerine; 2 ozs of cheese; 8 ozs of sugar; 1 lb of jam a month. I see from today's paper that whale-meat is to be put on the market shortly. So there's a nice prospect: whale-meat rissoles!

To turn to these books. I confess I have not got very far with the Washington Irving yet. I keep the book by my bedside as I find it makes an excellent night-cap: I usually start to fall asleep before I have read two pages! As for 'The Arch of Triumph': I regret to have to tell you, old lad, that I have read three chapters and can endure no more of it. Sordidness for its own sake I cannot stomach. I do not object to an author referring occasionally to the seamy side of life, but from what I have read, Remarque is not aware that there is another side. The story starts brightly with the central character preventing a woman from throwing herself off a bridge. He leaves her in rather a hurry to perform an illegal abortion. The patient dies so he decides to visit the nearest brothel. I had to grit my teeth to get this far, but when I reached the part where the author commences his meditation on urinating I burst into tears and had to put the book down. Am beginning to sense a divergence taking place in our literary predelictions, Courtney. One can understand a switch from P.G. to G.B.S., but the switch from P.G. to E.M.R. can only result in a blown out fuse (in my case, anyway).

Again, there is your enthusiasm for the music of Wagner. I am sure it is great stuff, but candidly I shy away from it. On the whole it seems to smack of supermen, storm-troopers, and great big empire-builders. For profound music I prefer Beethoven, who incidentally, has a delicious sense of humour which occasionally comes through. (e.g. 3rd movement of the 'Eroica'.) Heard any Rossini yet? He said the Tannhauser overture would sound the same backwards!

Finally, I suppose I must say something about this romance between Bobby and Dolly. It touches my finer emotions; in fact, I think I shall send them a wreath or something when the Great Day dawns and the wedding bells ring out. I note that all young people of my age appear to be thinking of Love. I don't know if you remember the three sisters I used to know at Lynchburg, but I received a card recently saying, 'Dr and Mrs Edwards request the horror of your presence at the marriage of their daughter. . . etc. etc.' For myself, I intend to remain an unrepentant bachelor, old lad. I may wed an heiress when I'm fifty, but even this is doubtful.

P.S. Desmond has had two court martials and is still in jail at Colombo. He would appreciate a letter.


*December 10th 1946*

Courtney old lad,

Yesterday was my 21st birthday: a quiet uneventful

day, as I would have wished it to be. I think it was Swift who said, 'A wise man never wishes to be younger', though one doesn't have to be wise to feel this way at 21. By the same token, he might have written, 'A wise man never wishes to be young.' And this is how I feel. At my age, I find it is very difficult to persuade anyone to take me seriously.

Now, regarding the enclosed Constitution: I think it is admirable, but if you have any amendments you would like made, let me know. Of course I have drawn it up because of Wilbur's idea to register the Square Peg Club as a legal entity so that when you have been appointed Vice Chairman or something, you will be able to come over here on a business passport. As far as I can see, this is the only way of getting round the passport difficulties you mentioned in your last. I presume Wilbur has already written to you about it.

Wilbur, incidentally, is hard at it trying to secure a place on the stage, even if it is only the hind-legs of a pantomime horse! At the moment, he is tenaciously pursuing several possibilities, and last week he chased a famous producer all the way to Oxford, living on little more than pieces of dry toast. He has no time to write letters at the moment.

I want to make it plain, old lad, that there is no hope of my attempting an Atlantic crossing either before or after your intended visit. In the first place, one has to have a strong reason for leaving Britain at present. With the economic plight as it is, the nation is calling for 'manpower', 'production' and other distressing things of this ilk. Now, as a registered 'psychopath' it might be argued that the Ministry of Labour would not be interested in enrolling my services, and that they might look upon a one-way ticket to the States as the next-best thing to a deportation order. But even if this was so, there remains the insuperable problem of my health. It has certainly improved during the last few months, but the fact remains that any sustained over-excitement still sends me tottering to my couch. For the moment, then, I have ruled out all prospects of further peregrinations. As I said last summer, I've had enough of this recently to last me a lifetime.

With regard to Britain's present parlous plight; everyone seems to think it is the fault of the socialist government, the simple truth being that it is the inevitable aftermath of the war. They seem to be surprised that the fruits of victory have proved so sour: namely, food shortages, fuel cuts, high taxation and ubiquitous misery. The Labour government, by the way, does not constitute a communist threat, as you seem to think, as the British people like the American, are too anti-any-sort-of-government by nature and tradition to put up with a totalitarian system: too individualistic, if you like. On the other hand, a communist system is temperamentally suited to the bovine hordes of Russia and China, and western capitalist apologists should bear this in mind. I hasten to add that I don't mean to endorse the methods of the abominable Stalin as Shaw seems to do; I am speaking solely about the Communist organization.

Since you tell me I am a cynic I have looked up the word in the dictionary, and it simply says, 'a morose man', a most inadequate description. I prefer Oscar Wilde's, 'A Cynic is a man who knows the price of everything and the value of nothing.' And I am certainly not this. Yet you will be gratified to hear that nearly everyone I know says I am a cynic.

I don't see how you can call me a cynic on the strength of that passage in the Poona essay. You also say, "You cannot classify human beings like postage stamps"; a criticism with which, as a professed caricaturist, I must profoundly disagree. I accept that my essay is something of a thumb-nail sketch, but I like to think that it reveals by way of its clear-cut delineation some very poignant truths.

On the perennial subject of cartoons: I am always pleased to get your ideas, but please have some consideration for the poor artist, old lad! You know how I hate drawing machines: they are bulky uninteresting objects. What I want is *space* and vast vistas of perspective; and I want subjects satirizing the empire-builder, on land, on sea,



DC–J

in the air, in jungles, deserts, village streets, splendid
gardens, and on the top of mountains. Also at the foot of
pretentious statues and war memorials, but not, laddie, in a
stuffy laboratory! You say that the cartoonist Thurber is
almost blind? I did not know this, but I might have guessed it
from his drawings. It's a pity that our tastes in this field are
so divergent. I don't mind telling you that Wilbur is having
difficulty in selling my work outside the office of one
intelligent editor. It's what I expected: it's too progressive
for them.

I agree with you wholeheartedly about 'programme
music'. Of course there are some pieces of descriptive music
that cannot be misrepresented, such as Debussy's 'L'après
midi' which could only be a summer landscape. Then ballet
music is a case apart as it was composed expressly for visual
illustration. Lastly, there is Walt Disney's immortal 'Fantasia'. It is much more than a cartoon ballet, of course; it is
*visualized music,* and he did it so enchantingly that he elevated
that wonder of modern science — the animated cartoon, into
the realm of fine art.

Now, I can already hear your protests. The Beethoven
'Pastoral' sequence. . . And I do not deny that this was the
weakest part of the film, and mawkish to a degree. But I treat
it as an exception; a joke — a witticism at the expense of
Greek mythology, and with its cute gags and coy sentiment,
a sample of Walt Disney — children's entertainer. The
music is so much greater than the images that the two do not
mix. Inevitably, this was the sequence that the unsympathe-
tic critics picked on. Yet even here amidst the pipe-playing
Pans and centaurs the essential Nature mysticism of Disney
is discernible. But if it is only discernible here, it is
overwhelming in the 'Nutcracker' sequence. If this is not a
mystical vision, then it is nothing.

By the way, you say your favourite Rossini overture is
'La Goosi Golda'? This is a new one on me, in fact I have
never even heard of it. According to my list, Rossini never
wrote an opera of this name. But I'll write to Vere about it.

P.S. No news from Desmond.

Courtney old lad,

A happy New Year, and all that! And may it see your emancipation from that leper colony, Emory, and our long-delayed meeting. I well know that one of the main ambitions of your life is to get out of the State of Virginia, and it is great news to hear that it is now within your reach. You may rely on Wilbur and myself to see that your stay in England will be interesting.

Not much to report since I last wrote, except that Desmond has been incarcerated in the notorious detention barracks at Lucknow. Do not censure him for this failure, old lad. He was driven to it, I do assure you. It is criminal to send a person of his sensibility on British Indian Service.

Wilbur's latest brainstorm is to produce open-air theatricals in Hyde Park, and he is going to present his plan to London County Council this week. Personally I can't think of a worse time for thinking about open-air theatricals (I haven't felt warm for weeks), but no one can say Wilbur doesn't try.

As for myself, although I am at present hibernating and leading the life of a veritable recluse, I am never bored. When I am not working away at the drawing board, I am reading books or washing dishes. (We find we have much more to eat since Mother dismissed the maid.) Mother is good company although she disagrees with almost everything I say. After I have finished expounding some deep thought, she is inclined to look up brightly and say, "I don't think I'll have frilly curtains in the end bedroom."!

The book I am reading at the moment is Somerset Maugham's 'Round Dozen', and I must acknowledge the story, The Creative Impulse, as being a masterpiece of humour. In it, he arrives at the home of some sophisticated female novelist in time for tea, and enquires, "Is Divine Service being held this afternoon?" I have this feeling that Maugham is never really at home except when writing about duchesses, peers, aesthetes, and other delicate blooms of hot-house society. But the best fictional character he ever created is that suave, evasive, cunning personage, so perfectly mannered and so detached — W. S. Maugham.

I confess I fell hook, line and sinker for that Rossini gag! A con man would have no difficulty in extracting a thousand from me (if I had it) for the manuscript score of a non-existent Rossini overture. I have just purchased records of Beethoven's 'Pastoral', Bruno Walter conducting.

February 20th 1947

Courtney old lad,

The postman has just shoved another missive from you through the frozen letter-box, and as it has just struck four o'clock which means we are allowed to switch on, I think I'll switch myself on and despite my awful chilblains, try and answer it. Trust me to come back from India to the coldest British winter for 106 years.

I am naturally delighted to hear that you have obtained your passport, old lad. Let's hope you have the same success with the visa. If not, I suppose we can put Wilbur's wheeze into operation.

Look, old boy, I don't want to strike a discordant note, but it seems to me you do nothing but over-eat yourself. There was some exuse for that ham at Christmas, I suppose, but I'm afraid I can't feel any sympathy for these doughnuts. I think it's revolting, and I must warn you that you won't be able to do it when you get here! The days when Bertie Wooster used to sally forth in his 'soup and fish' to the tune of a butler banging away at a gong have irretrievably passed. Nowadays, if we get the soup we don't get the fish, and vice versa. To illustrate this I enclose a news-cutting headed, 'Plans For Princess Are Off'. And what amazes me is that in the England of 47 they should ever have been on! So the answer to your question: "Do you English feudals still persist in taking your meals in tuxedos? If so, I'll bring mine.

140

If not, I'll bring my brown seersucker." — is, by all means bring your brown seersucker; it'll stand out well against my soup-stained smoking jacket.

The big news this week is that two days ago I received a 'letter' from Desmond in two envelopes and covering twenty pages written the day after his release from the glasshouse at Lucknow. His experiences therein were certainly something to write home about. He does not mention the letter you wrote him, though he says my own and Wilbur's letters kept him going and "saved me from suicide. If that is an exaggeration, it is not much of one." He says that because of my inflammatory letters, the Square Peg Club became something of a legend among the staff who had the privilege of censoring them. In the final interview, the Commandant said, "I don't know who this chap is who writes you about empire-builders, but you can tell him from one of them that I think he's screwy." Damn funny, what!

Desmond is back at Ceylon and may be home this year, though not in time to meet you, I'm afraid.

No, I have not read 'Of Human Bondage'; I've never been able to get hold of it. Liverpool Library was blown up by a bomb, and none of the smaller ones have it on their shelves. Incidentally, I hear Paul Henreid is playing whats-is-name in the film version which will probably be a travesty.

## The Square Peg Club.

*April 9th 1947*

Courtney old lad,

I am sure you will agree with me that this is very distinguished notepaper. The crest, if you remember, was your inspiration. Liverpool had to be combed to find a craftsman willing to engrave it for me, and it has taken him since October to do it.

I bounced out of bed this morning (can you see me bouncing?) and landed painfully on the horns of a dilemma. I found the enclosed missive from the United States Lines waiting for me, and as you will see, they charge the same monstrous sum as Cunard. Having done all my travelling 'expenses paid', I had no idea it was going to cost you £43 to cross the Atlantic each way. No wonder you intimated that you would attempt the journey on a raft with a long pole if there was half a chance you would get here.

As a matter of fact, I doubt whether the berth they are offering on this garbage scow will be much better, but there does not seem to be anything else sailing at present, does there? As the enclosed press-cutting make clear, berths on all lines, except the very expensive, are booked up till the end of this year, and even so, have long waiting lists for them.

It is all very frustrating, especially the fact that none of these vessels sail from Liverpool: all they do there, apparently, is unload dried eggs. You will see that the wallah finishes with the cryptic remark, "We will take up this matter with our London office." What this means, if anything, I don't know and your guess is as good as mine. Does he mean, perhaps, that boats occasionally dock at Liverpool which do *not* unload dried eggs? And if they do, why does he have to contact his London office to find out about it? It is all very confusing. Myself, I don't see why they can't unload fewer eggs at Liverpool: let Southampton do a bit of it, then they'll have room at Liverpool to unload a few people. It's a damned nuisance that you'll have to come all the way from Southampton, but there's no help for it. The only alternative, old lad, is to disguise yourself as a box of dried eggs, and I don't really think it's a practical possibility.

Now, briefly, here is an outline of the programme Wilbur and I have worked out for you starting from the moment you dock at Southampton (and let me know your sailing date as soon as you can, old boy). He and I will meet

you, and we will all repair to his London flat, assuming he
has got one by then. He knows London like the back of his
hand, and while we are there he will be undisputed Master of
Ceremonies. We will spend at least a week in town
meandering about, listening to the chimes of Big Ben, and so
forth. Among the items he has planned are: a trip up the river
to Oxford, a visit to the Royal Academy, and seats in the
gallery of the House of Commons. He also plans to have all
our pictures taken at his friend's studio. Subsequently, you
and I will come up here to Broad Leas where we will remain
impounded, enjoying perhaps an occasional game of
croquet, until the day of your departure arrives. . . . So you
see, things are beginning to shape up at last!

Today is the first real day of Spring. Shoots are
shooting, and buds are visibly budding under the sun's rays
which are beaming down on me as I sit on the lawn wearing
my new Donegal tweed sports jacket. I hope that very soon
you will be sharing such simple delights with me, though one
can never tell what the weather is going to do here.
Yesterday there was a dismal gale blowing. However,
whatever its faults the English weather always keeps you
interested and is not conducive to mental apathy like the
torrid heat of India.


*April 20th 1947*

Courtney old lad,

I have lost no time in placing the facts unequivocally
before this chap Casey. I told him that unless you could
furnish evidence of return transport, you would not get your
visa, and the enclosed letter is the result. In it you will see
your name is down for a berth on a freighter sailing from
Southampton sometime in September. I hope this is all that
is required. It is the best I can do; in fact, only a relative of
the Captain of the Queen Elizabeth could hope to do any
better. I suggest you send this letter to the big-wigs in

Baltimore and see what they say.

Now, it is no use talking about "the advantages of letting things work out for themselves", old boy, because there aren't any. Nothing would work out if we didn't make it, I do assure you. You are about to set foot in England in the year 1947 when theatre tickets, hotel reservations, almost everything you can think of has to be booked a month beforehand. If Wilbur did not start arranging the London tour about now, nothing would go smoothly. You are already aware of the inordinate trouble involved in obtaining a passport and securing a return passage. Most things give the same sort of trouble and are subject to unbelievable delays due to the infelicitous fact that this country has almost been brought to a standstill. Things are getting worse not better, and in my view it is a good thing you are coming this year as next year there will be a hundred new restrictions.

I heartily sympathize with your distaste for reception committees and organized games, old lad, and believe me, Wilbur and I will try to be as casual as possible. We will *not* slap you on the back, so there is no need to wear those spiked suspenders you mention; we will not carry your bags for you but merely give you instructions to put them in the back of the car. There will be no brass band playing Sousa marches, and there will not be the slightest sign of coloured bunting anywhere. It will almost certainly be raining, and in the event, you will find yourself feeling damn glad that there is someone to meet you. Wilbur is coming up next week to finalize our plans.

I apologize if my letters have seemed perfunctory lately. I put it down to the glorious Spring which has at last arrived. It has a languid effect on me and I don't seem able to cogitate. It is a time for taking deep breaths and nipping out onto the croquet lawn to improve one's hoop shots, not writing letters. Also, with your arrival almost imminent, I feel all discussions can be shelved until they can be continued verbally.

P.S. Peter will not be around. As I type these lines he is

approaching Haifa as a deck-hand on some R.N. tub-o-war.

*May 27th 1947*

Courtney old lad,

Wilbur has just left after spending the week-end here, and I am in a state of collapse! Of course, he is an unusually restless person, constitutionally incapable of sitting still for more than five minutes, and in three hectic days he has managed to reduce me to a quaking wreck.

So much so, that I have reluctantly come to the conclusion that a week in London with the indefatigable Wilbur as my host would render me a spent force for the rest of the summer, assuming it had no more serious effect on my struggling health. I can't face it, Courtney old lad. If there was one chance in ten that I might meet the challenge I'd chance it, but there isn't. All of which means that after all I said in my last letter, I shall not be on the quay when you steam into Southampton.

I have yet to inform Wilbur of this decision, but when I do I will arrange for him to meet you by himself. You will then be at his mercy for a few days while he shows you the town. He will, I know, insist that you put up with him (assuming he has got a flat by then). You will find him refreshing and unique, if somewhat scatterbrained and a menace to society. You could phone me from London.

In place of my London jaunt I am planning a fishing trip to Wales. The scenery is superb, and I know I should enjoy a holiday in Wales more than in that human ant-hill, London. Fishing is a leisurely sport and would take us into beautiful and quiescent places. I am as convinced that a Welsh fishing holiday in your company will set the seal on my recuperation as I am that a London visit under Wilbur's direction would indubitably render me inanimate. Anyway, tell me how it strikes you? It would last for about two weeks, and we would stay at some guest house. Mother would accompany us.

145

I have bought a book called, 'Let's Go Fishing' and I confess that before I read this book I was rather dubious about the whole scheme. I felt it might be somewhat callous to move into Wales to vandalize the local fish stocks, but now I have discovered that we can count ourselves lucky if we even *see* a fish. I don't mean that there are very few fish in Welsh rivers; on the contrary, they are bursting with them. It's just that fish are no fools and very elusive to the amateur manipulator of rod and line. The writer of this book, who once caught a fifty pound pike, says the art of fly fishing is not to let the fish catch sight of you, which is especially difficult in the case of trout as they can see round corners. He describes how he once wriggled down a hill covered with thistles on his stomach so as not to let a school of chub catch sight of him. I don't suggest that we go this far, in fact I know we won't. But it shows you what we could be up against.

Wilbur, I must tell you, has now decided that it is problematic whether he will ever come to much as an actor, and is harnessing his inexhaustible energies to this interesting estate agent's job. In short, he has chosen to sacrifice the nebulous pursuit of Art for the concrete pursuit of money. As he put it to me: if the price of getting onto the stage is starvation, he would sooner be in business. The trouble is that the appetite for riches grows with what it feeds on; the ultimate danger being that one can turn into a Philistine. But there is not, I admit, any answer to Wilbur's argument that no opportunity has come his way. He has tried his utmost, yet every time has drawn a blank.

Desmond's aspirations, on the other hand, are still in the ascendant. He has written a play, a copy of which I received last week. It concerns an inventor who discovers a death-ray, and decides to use it to murder all the world's atomic scientists. It is a trifle melodramatic. I have sent him a criticism of it.

The croquet lawn beckons.

**Courtney eventually arrived early one morning in July. I went to the station to find him "out on his feet" having taken an overnight train from Southampton. He brought the ham. Wilbur joined us one week-end. We spent two weeks in North Wales during August but did not catch any fish. We did not do much writing either. It was very hot, and the rivers around Bettys-y-Coed were down to a trickle. He departed for London and Wilbur, while Mother and I returned to Broad Leas to find a seven-foot sunflower by the front door and the croquet lawn looking like part of Deolali.**

*September 1st 1947*

Courtney old lad,

So once again it must be the written word.

Well, laddie, I got your letter accompanied by a note from Wilbur this morning. Things seem to have gone as smoothly as could be hoped. Mr Pickwick used to have the same sort of trouble moving about England in a coach, and things haven't changed much. Write me more fully when you get home. Did you, for instance, see Anne Hathaway's Cottage? Did Wilbur behave himself? Did you meet Phyllis? And what happened in London? I shall have to go down and visit W. in his new flat; my curiosity is getting the better of me.*

Mother expressed amazement when I told her you had asked Wilbur over to the U.S. next year. She said you were glad to see the last of him after that week-end. I tried to point out that the strength of the Club lay in the fact that the members kept pulling each other's hair rather than patting each other's backs, but she can't see it. She also thinks you were bored to death from the moment you arrived. I scoffed at this and said you were languid not bored, and you had many silent interests! But she still believes that if we had kept shuttling back and forth through the Mersey Tunnel,

*I never did. G.L.

everything would have been a lot better.

You did well to come over this summer as goodness-knows what things will be like this time next year. Next month the petrol ration for private cars is being stopped indefinitely which means the Welsh trip would be scratched for a start. I have got my bicycle out again but the wheels are wobbly. It goes like a bird — with a broken wing!

P.S. I hope you didn't have a bad time on the voyage.


*September 20th 1947*

Courtney old lad,

Received your voluminous letter this morning. You must have worked at it for hours, leaving those young intellectuals at the Rustburg Academy to solve their own geometric problems. This large sheet of paper does not indicate that I am going to try to equal it: it doesn't indicate anything.

If you were here, I could not extract half so many words from you in a whole day. During the morning you would play Beethoven recordings (a solecism I find hard to condone), and during the afternoon you would collapse into an armchair with a Huxley novel, breaking the interminable silence with one or two subtle smiles. When it was time for bed you would suggest going for a walk!

If there were two things that stood out during your visit, one was your leaning towards Prussian Culture and the other your sloppy way of eating! The first is o.k. Keep it up. But the second is deplorable and is almost certainly the cause of your lassitude. Myself, I am rapidly becoming a vegetarian. Shaw was right when he said we dig our graves with our teeth. If potato rationing comes in, I think I will burn my boats and take out a vegetarian ration book. In exchange for the minute meat and bacon rations you get twelve extra ounces of cheese and two ounces of fat.

Your description of the Wilbur-Phyllis set-up in

London is most illuminating. I now have a good picture of Phyllis and what she means to Wilbur. I had some such idea before, of course, but now it is confirmed. I was never quite sure what to make of Wilbur's explanation of Phyllis.

I could not agree more with your character study of Wilbur. You say you are genuinely fond of him. Of course I am too, and have been ever since he told a guffawing Provost Sergeant to stop laying eggs back in 1944. But he is hopelessly volatile, as you say; and for this very reason there is no cause for you to be perturbed about his intention to visit you. In all probability he has already forgotten about it and is planning a porpoise-hunting expedition off the Isle of Skye for next summer. In any case, it is going to become increasingly hard for anybody to get out of England. I keep getting ecstatic letters from him describing the new decorations of his Hyde Park flat. He is throwing a big house-warming party next month when evening dress will be worn. Sounds awfully respectable.

Desmond expects to leave for home very soon. He says he received our card from Bettys and is sorry to have missed you. He has been intending to write you for the past six months. He says Wilbur sent him a pocket edition of 'Punch' to keep his spirits up when in jail!

He also says he is working on a three act farce to be called 'The Possessive Case'. The principal character is a shy young man who, through frustrated love, develops an ultra-possessive attitude towards his personal belongings; his cigarette case, his hair comb, etc. Of course, there's a psychiatrist in it. This brand of tomfoolery sounds a bit coy for Desmond, I think.

So you began to feel sea-sick before you got on the boat?

I see Chaplin's new film, 'Monsieur Verdoux', has been banned from your country, though not here. I shan't miss it as it must be good.

P.S. I presented Doyle* with those photos. All he said was that he had got his 'blocker' on.

*the old gardener

Courtney old lad,

Many thanks for your essay and accompanying letter received this morning. But don't hit the keys of your typewriter so hard, old lad; the middle has come out of all the 'o's and 'b's and I can see through to the other side.

You've obviously put a lot of work into this essay; it is well thought out, and by and large, lucidly expressed. The only point I would question lies in the first sentence. It is *not* generally agreed that we are living in an era of cultural sterility, etc. No modern artist or art critic, of whatever branch of the Arts you choose, would agree that he is an exponent of a sterile culture.

Be that as it may, my concern is not with your argument but with your style of writing, which for me is too formal. Even the title exemplifies this fault. Should I happen to see something in my newspaper headed 'The Essential Abstraction', my instinct would be to turn the page in search of the cartoon. My dear old lad, this title might have been thought up by an elderly university professor addicted to writing very dry and very long books on Cuneiform Writing in Ancient Egypt.

Then look at that second sentence in the third paragraph: 'But, paradoxically, even conceding that it is wholly culpable for the decline of art, the lightning advance of science has developed heretofore unequalled opportunities for appreciation and appraisal.' Straight from the professor's manual, old lad. I had to read it three times to get the gist. Then hard on its heels, while the reader is still reeling from the blow, comes: 'Everything susceptible to adequate analysis is reduced to formalized equations of cause and effect.' I bet you got a kick out of writing that one!

My criticism then, is a call for a little of the old Courtney sardonic wit mixed in with the profundities, because at present, old boy, you might have a white beard ten feet long!

I have a positive suggestion to make. Why not write a serious essay on the work of P. G. Wodehouse? It's never

been done, at least, not adequately. I don't count that essay
by Orwell: he is too mundane to appreciate the subtleties of
P.G.'s art. For instance, he picks out one of those passages in
which Bingo is pleading with Bertie. You know the sort of
thing: "Bertie, we were at school together!" etc. etc. Then he
says, see how Wodehouse subscribes to the Old School Tie
moral code. . . Or words to that effect!!

Anyway, I hope you will give the idea some thought.

In case you do, here are a few random thoughts of my
own on the subject after reading his post-war publications.
As he has written over forty novels, it is not surprising that he
has nothing new to offer. In fact, you could say he has written
the same novel with variations, using the same stock
characters, over and over again. Something, incidentally,
that no other writer could get away with. This is not true of
his short stories which I have always thought superior to his
novels. P.G. is essentially a miniaturist. As he has no ideas or
characters in need of development, the scope of the novel is
wasted on him.

Having read 'Full Moon' and 'Money In The Bank', I
am prepared to stick my neck out and say that he is only
continuing to write because he is addicted to it. While he was
interned it is understandable that he would work away at
something to keep his spirits up, and I suppose it is arguable
that a similar effect might be induced in the reader. From the
purely artistic viewpoint, though, these stories are
uninspired and mechanical. It would have been better if his
reputation had been allowed to rest on his pre-war works.

P.S. I showed Mother your essay. She said she thinks
you are "a very serious boy"!

*November 13th 1947*

Courtney old lad,

Thanks for your hastily-scrawled note which arrived
this morning.

So you want a criticism of the ideas in your essay? The enclosed letter from Desmond to whom I sent it following his return home on 31st, should satisfy you completely. The two of us seem to take opposite views. He likes your style but is critical about your contentions, while I applaud your contentions but deprecate the pedantic way you express them. I hope you will not take either of us too seriously.

Desmond is going to Paris to spend two weeks with his uncle. He is then coming up here when Wilbur will join us. Wilbur phoned me last night to find out where Desmond had got to. But he also said he had definitely made up his mind to visit you next year as he can't find enough to eat in London.

Mother didn't read the essay. Her appraisal of you is based on your behaviour last summer. Can't give you any examples, but you do rather discourage levity, you know. . . Here's one; the best I can think of at a moment's notice. Let's say Mother puts a plate of spinach on the table for supper, and I gleefully commend the dish finishing with the innocuous words, "There's nothing I like better than a good dish of spinach!" In all probability you would sit back, pass a napkin over your mouth in an attempt to conceal a smile, and murmur, "W-e-e-ell, good for you!" in a tone that I can't possibly describe (faintly mocking, I suppose). Of course, it's like a blow on the back of the neck with a monkey wrench to the enthusiastic spinach-lover; and though I have chosen spinach as the theme as I can't think of a better one, you are inclined to 'throw the switch' in the face of any show of enthusiasm or high spirits. Of course, I wouldn't have you change this charming characteristic, but it *is* disconcerting, and does give you an air of solemn detachment.

I was at last persuaded to visit the ancestral roost, not having seen my relatives for two and a half years. My grandmother is over eighty now. They showed no curiosity in my army experiences; studiously avoided the subject, I thought. I remarked to my father that grandfather, to judge from his old books, was very well read in theology. I asked him if he had ever discussed the subject with him. "It's all above my head," came the reply. "I prefer a fast car and a camera myself."* Which remark illustrates the unavoidable fact that my mind functions on a different wave-length from my father. He has a radio concealed behind the oak panels in his cottage, but he was soon asleep and snoring loudly after I had switched on a philosophical talk by Lord Samuel.

As you know, Mother and I also disagree about most things, though this is offset by the fact that we share the same temperament. As a basis for domestic harmony I think the latter is far more important than intellectual acquiescence. Intellectually she was completely dominated by her father, a successful business man and local big-wig who died before I was born. She hero-worshipped him to the point of adulation with the unfortunate result that all her standards and moral judgements are those of a strait-laced Victorian.

For God's sake don't feel you have to provide Christmas dinners for the entire Club! If you are sending Wilbur something, divide his order by four. I myself will fare quite satisfactorily on my nutmeat brawn on toast. Did I tell you I have registered for vegetarian rations?

P.S. I will read 'Cakes and Ale' even if it upsets me.


*Monday, December 15th 1947*

Courtney old lad,

Plenty to write about this week.

Desmond duly arrived last Monday night. I was walking to the station and met him half way. Great to see him again: he has lost some weight but is just as nonchalant as ever. The arrangement was for Wilbur to come with him, but unforeseen obstacles arose keeping the London Terror at bay till Friday night. So we had four days to talk things over.

A few minutes before Wilbur rang on Friday to say he had reached Liverpool, Peter rang from Plymouth to

*"a fast car, a fast woman, and a camera" would have been a better answer.

announce that he was home from his travels and could we meet him at Lime Street at 1.30 a.m. Desmond had some demob petrol coupons which would supply the fuel, but unfortunately neither of us had a driver's licence. I told Peter it all depended on Wilbur, and he hadn't turned up yet. As things worked out, he jumped at the chance of a midnight drive, and at twenty past one we found ourselves at the station being accosted by a policeman who thought — probably because of Wilbur's deer-stalker — that we were a gang of spivs who had come to collect a consignment of black-market turkeys. We allayed his suspicions, however, and Peter duly appeared, looking bronzed and fit even in the yellow fog lights. We drove back through the Tunnel with Wilbur blowing the wind-horn, which in the cavernous emptiness sounded like something out of 'Tannhauser'. The three of them left for London in the car at 7.30 this morning. It is now 4 p.m. and Mother is still in bed!

Wilbur and Desmond ganged up on me over the week-end. (Peter was out most of the time with the lads of the village.) They are trying to drag me out of my 'cave' and get me gallavanting about the countryside soaking up 'experience'. Desmond is all for lots of experience; he doesn't seem to be able to talk about anything else — except chicken farming. We were trying to think up some desultory occupation for him which will rake in the doubloons without infringing his time or taxing his energy. The idea fell through when it became clear that Desmond's idea of chicken farming is a leisurely stroll down to the coop with a bucket of feed once a day.

Wilbur accused me of "wasting my youth" and living in my imagination. His recipe for making the most of it seems to be much the same as Desmond's: namely, to dash madly about in the West End of London. He does not seem to realize that my metabolic processes (if that's the right term) function a lot more slowly than his. I persistently refuse to visit him, because having seen what he is like in the country, I know that Wilbur in London would be a nightmare.

No one can say I didn't do my utmost to head him off

from visiting you next summer. I told him all sorts of things, bearing in mind that it's impossible to offend him. I said he was like a tonic — good for the patient in small doses but most upsetting when too much is taken. I pointed out that your father would be required to sign an avowal undertaking responsibility for him while in the U.S.A. Could anyone, I asked simply, be expected to take on responsibility for the behaviour of a penniless Wilburforce in New York City? Of course, he was undaunted, and retorted brightly that there was no problem since he would be wearing an undervest with pieces of valuable jewellery pinned all over it. So I tried again, saying that the price of a return ticket was £50, which your father might be obliged to pay. He said, no he wouldn't as he would get work the day he landed, whereupon Desmond chimed in saying he knew somebody who had told him finding a job in New York was next-door to impossible.

So it went on, with me growing more eloquent every minute. I explained that it was only the old Southern hosp. that had restrained you from pointing out these difficulties in the first place. I may have turned the scale, but it was you yourself who clinched the matter. Your letter arrived this morning, and I could not prevent Wilbur from leaning over my shoulder as I read it. "Who is the London Terror?" he asked. "You," I replied. "you'd better read it." I handed him the letter, and he did so. He didn't say anything, but he looked rather thoughtful for a while and did not refer to the subject again. I don't think you have anything more to worry about.

My last words to Desmond were to urge him to write to you. I said you were a lonely intellectual in a land of popcorn eaters.

Almost forgot to tell you that Vere is back in England too. He phoned this morning an hour or so after the others had gone; said he was demobbed a month ago and has been frantically trying to find work as an apprentice to an interior decorator. He asked me when he could come up and see me, and I said when Mother has settled down a bit! So it looks as if he will be the next visitor at Broad Leas.

Courtney old lad,

You will see I am writing you from Desmond's abode at Bedford, having arrived last Friday at 5 a.m. What had happened was this. Vere had been spending the week at Broad Leas when due, I suspect, to boredom he suddenly decided he would like to take the Thursday night train down to Bedford to meet Desmond. I agreed to accompany him, though not without some misgivings. For a start, part of Vere's plan was that our appearance was to be a surprise, and I could foresee that Desmond's first impression of Vere might be a little warped if it was made in the cold light of dawn from his bedroom window, having been woken up by half a brick coming through the pane. Anyway, I well knew the futility of attempting to subdue one of Vere's impulses, so I resigned myself to the inevitable and the two of us duly boarded the night 'sleeper' at Liverpool. At about 4.30 just as we were approaching Bedford, Vere characteristically changed his mind. Neither of us had had a wink of sleep; he admitted the escapade had been a ghastly mistake, and he just wanted to go straight home, have a hot bath and go to bed.

Of course, at this point I put my foot down. I said it was not my responsibility that Desmond was due to be woken from his slumbers at 5 a.m., and I was damned if I was going to face the assignment on my own. Somehow I managed to drag him off the train, but both our tempers were in tatters, and after wandering aimlessly about in the freezing cold arguing for half an hour, Vere decided to take the next train for London. This he did at 7 o'clock, leaving me in a semi-coma huddled in the waiting room where I was gently collected by Desmond an hour or so later. It is now Monday, and apart from a frightful cold, I feel almost restored to my usual tottering self.

I think you will have formed a clear impression of Vere from the above narrative: the artistic temperament personified. I believe I told you he plans to become an interior decorator: in fact, he starts this week at the Brixton School of Building with a view to obtaining the required diploma.

When he arrived at Broad Leas, the first object to strike his eye was the Queen Anne writing desk in the lounge. He proceeded to eulogize about this till Mother brought in the tea trolley, whereupon his ecstatic eye turned to the china teaset. Minton? Spode, perhaps? I fear I did not follow the discussion closely enough to recapitulate here. But it must be said that despite his habitual aesthetic response to all and sundry, Vere is always vivacious and amusing. Hard to capture in words, of course, but here is an example for you. While he was listening to a Debussy recording, Peter lounged in after a game of golf and began to sort out his bag of clubs. After a few moments, Vere jumped to his feet and abruptly switched off the machine with the remark: "One cannot listen to music and watch Peter clean golf clubs at the same time." He pronounces 'golf' like 'goaf', by the way. "But these goaf clubs do have an aesthetic 'feel' about them," he admitted a little later. When he was helping to lay the supper table, he put out four spoons in a serried row and four others in a haphazard heap, murmuring, "Constable and Picasso having a tête-à-tête."

All right: you may say he is just like Hayward in Maugham's book, but unlike Hayward, he does it all with a twinkle in his eye! His responses are always so superbly in character — so beautifully put, that only a born humorist could do it.

Of course, the contrast here with Desmond is marked, and I am impatient to discover how they react to each other. Desmond has virtually no aesthetic sense at all, especially in the case of music. He actually thought Debussy was some kind of salt! While he was a Broad Leas I tried him on Chopin, Smetana, and in desperation — a Beethoven overture. All to no avail. It meant nothing to him. He adamantly maintains that music is not self-sufficient and needs some sort of spectacle to go with it. He was impressed by 'Fantasia'. When I asked him if he thought Beethoven wrote his symphonies for the ballet, he said that he thought concert-goers were being hood-winked!

To some extent he suffers from inadequate education. You deplore your own lack of education, but compared to Desmond you are an Aldous Huxley. He has been trapped in the Army for four years, of course, but this cannot excuse his seeming indifference to serious reading. His home is full of good books which belonged to his father, yet he evinces little interest in them. Oddly enough, Desmond's father was a regular army officer, a doctor in the R.A.M.C. and apparently a man of some taste. He had a nice set of Corot repros.

Desmond's negative interest in the Arts inevitably limits his scope as a writer, and I suppose must sap his self-confidence. It is probably the cause of his disinclination to try his hand at an essay. I suggested he might follow your example, but he argued that anything he might produce would have been done a thousand times before by better men than he. I retorted that this cannot be true as every generation has new contemporary problems to think about. I also vainly argued that his work was bound to have originality as his thumbprint is different from anyone elses! A dubious analogy as all the workers in a factory have different fingerprints, which does not mean that they all have something original to contribute to English Literature. But he won't budge, and continues to fritter away his time making bed-side lamps out of pins and paper! We must do something to stimulate his creative powers, old lad, and I think it would be a good thing if you were to encourage him from your end. We must let him know that the two of us at least would be interested in reading his efforts.

Laddie, I opened that letter from you before Wilbur came into the room. I did my best to stop him reading it over my shoulder but it was hopeless. Don't worry: time followed by a conciliatory letter should smooth things over.

P.S. Mother likes Vere: she says he's a gentleman and knows how to behave!

Courtney old lad,

I am pleased to hear you have written a long letter to Desmond. You will find it a paying proposition as no matter how long it is, you will get one back double the length. All the snap-shots taken when he and Wilbur were here turned out to be under-exposed, I am sad to say. Better luck next time.

I also regret to report that both Wilbur and Desmond have refused to accept Vere as a member of the Club. They met at Wilbur's flat recently and went to see a play somewhere. Desmond writes that "he is obviously not a square peg", and Wilbur that he is "typical of the arty young men who drift about London." Naturally, when two such apparent opposites as they agree like this, I am shaken. Vere seems to have made the unpardonable error of trying to reform Wilbur, which amused Desmond no end but not the London Terror. I need hardly say that a reformed Wilburforce would be grotesque and intolerable; so perhaps they are right. Spotting the genuine psychopath is harder than picking the winner of the Grand National.

Now, I acknowledge with dutiful thanks the belated arrival of the food parcel. But there is a history with it which I shall now relate. Enclosed are a letter and a form from the Customs and Excise people. The letter speaks somewhat incoherently for itself. I replied that I lamented the fact that I must lose the goods because of the inefficiency of a woolly-minded American friend, and that as a vegetarian, I wished to make a special plea for the cheese. I said I would gladly pay the duty, but as the goods had been seized, I assumed it was impossible to do so. Actually, it was Millners' fault for failing to declare the cigarettes and stockings, not yours. On the label they had simply put, 'Food. $10'.

I then received the form, and you will notice that, by this stage, your parcel had gained the dignity of a number The content of the letter is so obscure that after several readings, I gave up the task as hopeless and had to play a

161

Chopin nocturne before I could tackle the problem. I caught at the phrase 'legal proceedings', and finally concluded that the point of the letter was to inform me that I could only obtain the parcel through extended litigation, the cost of which might well run into the hundreds. But I must have been wrong as you will see that on the printed form, which came next, the phrase 'legal proceedings' does not even appear. From this it seems that I can obtain the parcel simply by reaching for my wallet. Actually, it was Mother who reached for her handbag in the end as the stockings and cigarettes were for her use not mine.

The parcel arrived shortly afterwards, but I am left considering why these articles should be esteemed so much more valuable than 2 lbs of cheese and 6 tins of assorted prunes and apricots? One can live without cigarettes, and if a woman, can certainly get along without nylon stockings. There are wearable substitutes; but there are no substitutes for cheese which contains quantities of nourishing protein. Current English 'cheddar' is reputed to be concocted in a laboratory and is not made of butter or milk. God knows what it's made of! As a vegetarian, therefore, I am indebted to you for this sumptuous gift! Mother was happy to pay for the parcel which would have cost her more if bought at a store, assuming the goods were available.

Here are some suggestions for use when packing future food parcels for us.

Cheese. Any time you have an urge to send me a block of cheese, don't hesitate. To me, it is worth ten times the price you pay for it.

Tins of fruit. Quite unobtainable here, like the cheese.

Tins of beef. Excellent for the carnivores in the house, but they would prefer ham to beef. A tin of meat half the size of the one you sent costs 16 points, and the ration is only 24 a month.

Sugar. It is not as scarce as some other things and no packet of it from abroad has ever reached here intact. This one was half empty and had a ticket with 'Damaged' written on it. The damage had obviously been done by the man who wrote the ticket. It had been tipped out onto a dirty board of some sort and inspected for hidden gems.

Soap. Don't bother. We have more than we can use. I don't use much.

Puddings. We don't eat many cold sweets.

Tea. We don't need tea.

Now for Art. I have seen Chaplin's 'Monsieur Verdoux', and the more I think about it, the more I am convinced that he is the greatest exponent of high comedy since Molière. The script, the story, and the production were commonplace, and without Chaplin would have made a normal Hollywood melodrama. It was Chaplin's magic touch that transformed the piece. He called it 'A Comedy of Murders' — a startling subtitle. I saw nothing but burlesque in the film version of 'Arsenic and Old Lace', but Chaplin's play was entirely different. He was acting the part of a cold-blooded calculating killer. In the hands of Boris Karloff the result would have been horrific, yet by means of a subtle gesture here and there — the raising of an eye-brow, a grimace, or the fastidious use of slap-stick, he transformed the horror into absurdity, leaving you laughing hilariously. No one else could have done it. Perhaps it could be argued that the crime of murder is rather absurd compared to the mass homicide perpetrated by both sides in the war; and this, of course, is the moral of the tale, and the reason why the film has been banned in the U.S. I am sure Chaplin could do something with that absurd council for the suppression of un-American Activities.

P.S. So, if Stonewall Jackson hadn't got bogged down in White Oak swamp, General Lee would have destroyed the Federal Army. . .

*March 3rd 1948*

Courtney old lad,

I am sorry to hear that the flu germ has had a go at you,

163

and hope that you have now fully recovered and are once more back at the typewriter engaged in this headlong pursuit of nihilism with Desmond. Naturally I am delighted that you have turned out to be twin souls. All the same, I hope you can still spare me a few desultory lines occasionally despite the fact that I am not a dashed nihilist and am constitutionally incapable of emulating your icy detachment, which in your case is almost certainly due to a faulty digestion and in Desmond's is equally certainly due to innate indolence. We will never get him to write an essay, you know.

Have you noticed something about his letters; namely, that they're not confidential? It's as if he is letting off a display of intellectual fireworks for everybody to see. Bernard Shaw writes like this. You can't imagine Shaw confiding in anybody, can you? If he did, he would keep a copy and print it later as a preface to one of his plays! Desmond is part Irish, you know: perhaps it's an Irish characteristic.

To be serious, I do understand why you find Desmond so immensely sympathetic. But there is a superficial difference between you. In your case, the fact that you find life so meaningless is reflected in your languid personality: in Desmond's case, it is not. When he was here he wore a sort of track in the dining-room carpet walking round and round the table reiterating that he feels no enthusiasm for doing anything and is utterly miserable. Yet the whole time he had this happy ecstatic smile on his face! The truth is that he is one of the most genial souls I have ever known; temperamentally a complete stranger to depression and despair, I should have said. I have never seen him bad-tempered, and he is completely free of any sort of malice towards anything. If I ever feel annoyed with Desmond — and I hardly ever do — it is simply because he is never annoyed! He knows he has this characteristic, and he has written to me regretting it. "You," he said, "feel annoyed with empire-builders, wart-hogs, psychiatrists, princesses, etc., and so you feel inspired to satirize them." This is what he means by 'enthusiasm', and I suppose he is right. As he never feels stimulated either for or against anything for long, he is doomed to live in an intellectual limbo forever seeking some sort of momentary distraction.

I suppose he has told you all about the abortive engineering course? In case he has not, I hasten to add he chucked it up within a week; a good thing, in my view. He only entered for it because an industrial psychologist he consulted told him he had no special aptitude for anything except something vaguely termed 'manual acquisitiveness'. And as he had paid five guineas for this information plus a long list of things he was no good at (which he knew beforehand), he thought he had better have a poke at it. He told me he realized his mistake the next day when informed that all entrants were to bring boiler suits!

He spends most of his time in a never-ending discussion on what to do with himself. It's not that he is short of ideas, but he knows that after a week his interest will fizzle out and he will have to chuck it. As you know, he blames his introspective powers for this. He is always led to the negative — one might say, Oriental conclusion that all activity is futile. The purposeful man is like a dog chasing its own tail, and the wise man should do nothing. On the face of it, a rational explanation for his behaviour as all Desmond's explanations are. Yet I believe the true one should be sought elsewhere, namely in his temperament. Most people see Desmond as an incurable lazybones, and I am bound to say that after a great deal of probing, I have come to the same conclusion myself. Being such a high-powered rationalist his laziness presents itself as the end-product of a long and complicated ratiocination when the truth is the other way round. It is the laziness which inspires the reasoning process.

I am afraid he will never overcome this laziness, you know. He will just drift along until one day his money runs out and he will then be compelled to find some degrading job. All his intellectual potential will run to waste.

But enough of Desmond. As for Wilbur; I don't know whether he received your package. I have written to him three times lately about my drawings but have received no

reply. Perhaps he is peeved over my disinclination to visit
him. He is so proud of his new flat. There is to be a
tremendous party next month. Desmond says there are cases
of Bollinger 37 reputed to be on their way from Phyllis's
fabulously wealthy uncle: boxes of brandy, sherry, cider,
beer, whisky, gin. . . "One picks one's way past a great side
of pig, past a tremendous lump of cow." Hardly a suitable
haunt for a newly converted vegetarian!

Brock is all right. He's become a little tamer since you
were here. I have managed to train him so that he no longer
barks at the striking clock: a low growl is all we get now. But
poor old Doyle seems to be packing up all of a sudden. He
hasn't done anything in the garden for weeks. I went over to
his cottage yesterday, and it's pathetic to see how depressed
he is. He looks worn out. Of course he is 77. He is never
happy unless pronging things with a fork, and one can
imagine how he must feel now that he no longer has the
strength. Old age is much more of a terror to a man like
Doyle than it is to an intellectual. I doubt whether Desmond
will notice it!

P.S. The fruit cake was excellent, but did you put that
packet of cocoa in as a sly joke? On the side it says, 'Top off
with a mashmallow or a spoonful of whipped cream.'


*April 24th 1948*

Courtney old lad,

A hasty post-card from Desmond came this morning.
He is staying at a hotel in Woking, and writes, "Wilbur and I
spent week-end in canoe. Found lovely bungalow in orchard.
Buying tomorrow, if not sold."

Wilbur has been seeing a lot of Desmond lately. As you
know, he and his mother are incompatible and he is in a most
unsettled state. I haven't had a letter from him for weeks.
Wilbur had this to say: "I have just spent the week-end at
Bedford and have dragged the hapless Desmond away from

his mother for a week to go down to the Woking, Surrey district and find a new house. I have told him he is not to return to Bedford or London until he has found one, and he departed yesterday, full of misgivings." Wilbur does not like the Bedford semi which is rather poky, and I suppose would prefer Desmond to live closer to Town. This would also suit Monica. Peter, by the way, has been staying with Wilbur in London while taking some exam, and says he has simmered down a lot. I imagine myself that Wilbur is just the same but that Peter has become more tolerant towards him.

"I don't think I've told you before, but I am now a reporter for the Daily Advance. . ." One of these days I'll get a post-script on one of your letters, saying, "By the way, I was run over by a street-car last week and lost both legs." You write as though this new chapter in your career is of no interest. I for one am extremely interested and would like to hear something about it. You say you are not suited to the job? Why not? Too active and all that? If so, can't you get a post as a critic of some sort?

In return, I can tell you that I am to have a series of caricatures published in a magazine called 'Music Parade'. But as it is only issued six times a year and I am to be paid half a guinea each for the drawings, it is rather a futile assignment. I drew a set of ten caricatures in ten days; enough to last the editor for twenty months, at the end of which time I shall have earned the princely sum of five guineas!

If you think I might hope for further assignments on the strength of this one, they will have to come to me as I haven't the remotest indication where to look for them. There are no other music periodicals that might be suitable venues, so my only hope is a literary magazine, and Wilbur has tried the lot now.

As might be expected, my nearest and dearest have been showing signs of concern lately, and such comments as, 'What if Graham *never* sells anything?' and 'He can't go on drawing for *ever*, can he?' have been increasing. Everybody, including myself, has been getting worried due to my lamentable lack of sales; but for different reasons. Mother & Co. are worried because I am not showing signs of financial independance and thus qualifying for what she vaguely calls 'a normal life'. Whereas I am worried because nobody seems to recognize the value of my work. Mother wants me to find some other way of earning money and to relegate my cartooning to the status of a hobby. She is convinced that if it hadn't been for the war and I had stayed on at public school, I would now be one of the boys and out with Peter and the rest of 'em preparing myself for some high-powered career. As in Desmond's case, the argument never gets anywhere, and when I tell her that if the worst comes to the worst I would get a job as a night watchman, it usually ends abruptly.

Last Saturday, Mother and I went to the Playhouse, Liverpool, to see Bernard Shaw's 'Heartbreak House', and I've a lot to say about it. This is the first Shaw play I have seen, apart from the movie 'Pygmalion', and I don't think it gained much over the radio version. Three hours of concentrated talk is better heard in the relaxed atmosphere of your sitting-room; an arm-chair certainly helps. However, I thoroughly enjoyed it and could have taken another hour. Mother could not! She complained of a headache and buzzing in the ears after the first Act, and said she would have walked out at the end of the second if I hadn't been there. She said, "There's something about Shaw's plays that completely exhausts me. I begin to feel queer after a while. I think they're too wordy." Entirely different with me, of course. It's emotion I can't stand since my nervous breakdown. Any suspense; anyone going mad or anything, and I'm finished! I can listen to Shaw's emotional shams for hours.

I know the point of this play is that nothing happens — that the characters are just drifting inconsequently nowhere, yet I still think Shaw should have provided some sort of a plot, some peg on which to hang it. All that happens is that a burglar is caught in the second Act and a bomb explodes in the third, nearly blowing me out of my seat. The rest of the

time the actors come on in pairs, seat themselves comfortably, and talk. When they have said all they have to say, they
are replaced by two more. Shaw's method — or lack of
method — is particularly obvious in this play. He simply
puts two characters in together, and — like some cerebral
try-your-strength machine, tries to ring the bell with them.
When he succeeds, or when he knows he has failed, he
replaces them by another two. When he has shuffled up the
lot he brings down the curtain.

In 'Heartbreak House' I think he fails to ring the bell
more often than not. There is little of the sustained brilliance
one finds in his best plays. He succeeds when Shotover is
talking to the girl at the end of the second Act; and again
when her self-effacing father is analyzing Mangden's
worldly worth. Shotover is well up to the best Shavian
standard, and of course is G.B.S. thinly disguised. His
observations on senility are the most telling in the play. This
may have been because Shaw was beginning to grow old
himself: I don't know, but that line in the last Act struck me
as significant. ". . .merely echoes; my last shot was fired
years ago."

The acting was very polished although they might have
played with a little more humour. All Shaw's parts demand
over-acting. The flashes of sheer farce in this play — when
Hector enters dressed as a sheik, for instance — the actors
handled clumsily. After an earnest conversation, grown men
would suddenly burst into tears or be sent off to bed. These
incidents came as more of a shock than a surprise. Partly
Shaw's fault for being over-capricious perhaps; but if the
director had treated the play a little more farcically, the
production might have been improved.

P.S. If you want to read something *really* funny, try
Shaw's 'Misalliance'; overlooked, perhaps because there is
not much doctrine in it.

Courtney old lad,

The News Hound's typical day intrigued me immensely. I feel sure you have set foot on the first rung of your literary career. The only drawback to your job that I can see is this incessant climbing of the North Street steps. In fact, it may prove to be your downfall!

Yes, I have to agree with you; there is precious little Art about Shaw's plays, and from his writings I gather he is very much aware of this fact and regrets it. Say what he will against artists and what he will in favour of socialists, it is the artist whom he respects more than anybody. I notice this fact emerging all the time in his writings. As you say, Shaw knows precious little about 'form', and other professional dramatists are vastly more skilful in this field and at using other tricks of the trade. Yet the fact remains that his best plays are incomparably greater than theirs. Similarly, despite what Shaw will tell you, he is not a poet. He has in fact proved that to be a great dramatist one need not be a poet or much of an artist.

It follows that the essence of art is not artistry; it is the thought behind the artistry that really counts. The thought is striving for expression, and the artist uses the best technique at his disposal as a means of expressing it. Obviously the means must be skilful enough to present the thought, otherwise the work would be a failure, but essentially it is the quality of thought — the vision that matters. There are many second-rate artists who are first-rate technicians.

You say that Shaw the old man is dotty, and here I cannot agree with you, though there must be many who would. I don't think Shaw today is the least bit dotty; or rather, he is no more dotty than he ever was. His 'Everybody's Political What's-What?', written during the war, is surely one of his major works, and as an example of effective expression, is beyond the reach of criticism. His powers of expression have not diminished; neither has his wit, which is as sparkling as ever.

What has changed is that he is no longer able to
assimilate new ideas, so that everything he says which is
supposed to pertain to current affairs is a sort of anachron-
ism; it is what he thought about the subject thirty or forty
years ago re-hashed for the occasion. His views on the Soviet
Union are particularly out of date: he still sees it as an
adventurous new experiment in Marxist socialism when it
has become a ruthless dictatorship. He can't see Stalin and
his henchmen for what they are. But enough about Shaw. . .
the topic is inexhaustible.

A letter from Desmond describing in his meticulous
way the attributes of the bungalow at Shepperton-on-
Thames they have just bought. Has he written to you? His
letter-writing has been spasmodic lately due to house-
hunting, and will become even more so as they are planning
to move in in a few weeks.

June 8th 1948

Courtney old lad,

I have stirred up an interesting letter from Desmond. I
sent him one in which I quoted your remark that because of
'Hegelian evolution' (whatever that is?) he will eventually
tire of us, and that you see signs that the Club is beginning to
disintegrate. He writes: ". . .How I have longed for letters
from Courtney this last month or so. (Mind you tell him
this.) I have nothing left to tell him. He is fully cognizant of
everything that has ever happened inside my skull: I have
exposed the entire mechanism. I also suspect that there are
only insignificant parts of his cerebellum with which I am
not already acquainted. However, our two minds interact
with fairly interesting results, so when he next gives me a
mental jolt, I will resume the correspondence."

He is now at the new house at Shepperton. The day they
moved in, Wilbur turned up "adding to the confusion." He
goes on to say that he and Wilbur are off on a jaunt across

171

Europe in an old M.G. next week, so your foreboding regarding the Club would seem to be premature. A note from Wilbur seeming to confirm this escapade came by the same post. Airy optimism from Wilbur: minute details from Desmond who says that Wilbur is a lousy driver and will need a restraining hand. "He craves for thrills, and takes risks in the hope of having a minor accident." He seems to have had one in London recently. Desmond says that on his return he is going to start a one-man business called 'Glorified Chars Ltd. The Gentleman Cleaners'. . .! This contrasts oddly with Wilbur's remark that they are intending to start a Chinese restaurant together.

Wilbur has returned all my cartoons with some barbed words about my lack of commercial sense. Of course he is right. I should have stuck to the decision I came to 'when I was in Poona' and given up all aspirations for this kind of thing. I have decided to go in for book illustration, and am working on a set of drawings for Peacock's 'Headlong Hall'. English comic book illustration is now almost defunct whereas the magazines are choked with cartoons, most of them badly reproduced and far too small.

Magazines have killed more humorous artists than I can name. Emett, for instance, has had a drawing in 'Punch' almost every week for seven years, and with what result? He has become a National Institution. Name a worse fate if you can! What it means is that 'Punch' readers miss Emett's cartoon if it is not there but do not notice it when it is! Staleness and public disinterest is the prize for becoming a popular cartoonist, and I don't wish to enter the lists. 'Punch' incidentally, is totally out of date, and I hazard a guess that it is only the subscribers in the outposts of the Empire who want a link with home who keep it going.

Alright, so you still think Shaw is dotty, and he has always advocated dictatorship. . . Even so, I am certain the Utopian state he has in mind is not as inhumane as the Soviet set-up. It is described more fully than elsewhere in the 'What's-What?', and my misgivings are not based on any doubt that it might not be an improvement on the present constitution (democracy cannot work in the long run anyway) but on the conviction that the integrity of such a system could not be maintained. He describes how the rulers are to be selected by a foolproof system of panels and examinations, but what he cannot possibly know is that they will rule wisely and will not be corrupted by the power they wield. This is the fatal flaw in his system. There is no guarantee that the ideal will work out in practice.

For instance, although the state is to be a dictatorship, there will be certain licensed freedoms. Heterodox thinking and writing will be permitted in order to safeguard the progress of ideas. This is all very fine; the State must ensure the survival of any future Bernard Shaw with revolutionary bees in his bonnet, but can we really believe that any ideas the rulers profoundly disapproved of would not be suppressed? Of course we cannot. A new and better Bernard Shaw would assuredly have his licence to live revoked on the old-fashioned grounds of sedition as it is untenable to suppose that any absolute ruler would maintain a priviledge which could weaken his power.

This is the flaw in all socialist systems; they are based on the false premise that the State knows best and will not abuse its power. And this is why they are highly dangerous to people like ourselves — members of the Square Peg Club. We should either be executed or made to 'work', and I shudder at the prospect! I would be classed as a 'parasite', Desmond as a 'drone', and Wilbur as a 'public nuisance'. Shaw's Utopia makes no allowance for congenital drones. He stipulates that no person shall live on the labour of others unless unfit, and that all able-bodied people shall work a minimum of four hours a working day. He would not approve of a bee hive. Bertrand Russell, on the other hand, is more lenient. He realizes that there are some people to whom prison is less terrifying than work, and who are incapable of persisting at any regular employment. He makes allowance for them in his ideal State in the same way as he makes allowance for the blind, pointing out that they are few in number and should be granted a bare subsistance allowance which they could increase by working if they wanted to. He says that in a well-organized state, periods of work would be short and pleasant, and most people would want to be employed.

But whether we like it or not, it is obvious that the growth of socialism in Britain is inexorable and will continue, perhaps to a modified degree, even if the Tories regain office. The Tories would put the brake on socialism which has been developing alarmingly here since the war, and they could be depended upon to safeguard the rights of the individual. But I cannot see them returning while Churchill is still at the helm. At the last election, Shaw made the comment that Attlee would win because of his quiet manner, and it is true that his conversational mike-side manner compares favourably with Churchill's oratorical bombast. In wartime this sort of thing goes — *everybody* has hysteria, but not in peacetime when — to quote the old boy — "the crimson wings of war" do not o'erspread England's "green and pleasant land." I think somebody else was the author of the last bit.

*June 21st 1948*

Courtney old lad,

First, many thanks for the Chaucer which arrived just after I had gone out to post my last letter. Also another air-mail from you.

I don't know whether it struck you or not, but that line on the cover: 'A gorgeous rendering of the lusty stories of England's Rabelais' was typically American! I have read the Prologue, and there are some superb passages in it; really fine-grain humour. It must be one of the best examples of written caricature in English. But I think the adaptation into modern English is too thorough. Nicolson has ironed out all the old English words when he could have left many which would be perfectly understandable and would enhance the

Chaucerian flavour. Chesterton has explained this in two typical sentences: 'No reader minds meeting an old word, but is only bothered when he meets a new word. I mean, of course, a word that is new to him; a word that is old enough to be new.' The first line of 'Canterbury Tales' is, 'When that Aprille with his schowres swoote'. 'Swoote' is to rhyme with 'root' so cannot be changed to 'sweet'. All that need be done to this line is a footnote saying that 'swoote' means 'sweet'. But what does Nicolson do? He writes, 'When April with his showers sweet with fruit.' Ridiculous! There is no fruit in England in April — only forced rhubarb. Nicolson has no right to make Chaucer look a fool. I am consistently irritated by his thoroughness, but nonetheless I have to thank him for making the verse so readable.

Regarding the illustrations by Rockwell Kent: I will give you my candid opinion. (We never seem to agree over drawings!) All the figures seem to have rheumatism. As dummies depicting 14th century costume they are adequate, but not as visualizations of Chaucer's characters. None of them show any character at all: they are as dead as mutton.

To turn to your letter: your decision to renounce the world of the news-hound and become a cloistered philosopher is a good one. The role will suit you admirably. You ask me if Mother has made any more *bon mots*? Well, I've just read out a few sentences from your letter, and she has pronounced the following profundities. She said, "He couldn't have made a better choice. I think he will make a very good professor: he's getting to sound very much like one." I replied, "But he says here that he doesn't enjoy reading 'an embarrassingly large number of the world's best writers.' Surely that is inconsistent with the true professor?" "Oh, not it's not," she said. "He'll come to read them in time."

I also sounded out Peter on the subject, but his reaction was the opposite. He was completely fogged. He said, "Why doesn't he take a course in engineering and learn something?"!!

In one of your letters you mentioned G.K. Chesterton

— the only time you have ever referred to him. I think you said something to the effect that Chesterton's geniality disguises his lack of intellect. Quite wrong, in my view. He certainly had the brains to take on Shaw: the two of them exchanged gentlemanly blows for almost half a century. But while he was Shaw's equal in debate, he was distinctly his inferior as a creative artist. He is chiefly remembered for a handful of detective stories.

Yet, as I say, he is an excellent literary critic and has a rollicking sense of humour which you would no doubt call 'naïve'. You would be quite right: he is naïve. There is something naïve about all the best humour. The more adult you become, the less humour you seem to possess. It only takes a glance at Aldous Huxley to demonstrate the perils of intellectual maturity. He is so sober and serious that he can find nothing to laugh at. Somerset Maugham, I am glad to see, is laying down his pen with a smile rather than groan. His last novel, 'Catalina', is frankly trivial.

I have a suspicion that unless a writer is an agnostic, you consider him intellectually inferior. Though — Goodness-knows — no one who has read 'Ends and Means' could call Huxley an agnostic. G.K.C. is not an agnostic; he is an avowed Catholic. His arguments are based on Church dogma, and he defends them with a skill that no mere bishop could possess. I am not saying I agree with him. His attitudes are rooted in his belief in the virtues of the Common Man, and you know what I think about that! His attack on Shaw is basically that Shaw has never been able to understand the things the Common Man has always taken for granted. His book on Shaw is exactly what the Common Man would say about Shaw if his mental powers were multiplied by ten. He attacks Shaw for his presumption in aspiring to be a Super-man.

But don't let me put you off reading the book. It must be the most discerning study of Shaw that has ever been written. Before I began to read, I imagined that the picture presented would be as unlike Shaw as Chesterton is himself. But I was wrong. It is exactly like Shaw: it is only

Chesterton's judgement about what he sees that is disputable, and in some cases absurd. For instance — and this is perhaps the most absurd of the lot: 'One cannot imagine him (Shaw) inspiring any of his followers to write a war song or a drinking song or a love song, the three forms of human utterance which come next in nobility to prayer.' But to counterbalance this, I hasten to append: '. . .there does run through him this erratic levity, an explosion of ineptitude. It is a queer quality in literature. It is a sort of cold extravagance: and it has made him all his enemies.'

It did not need Chesterton's book to make me aware of Shaw's faults: they are mostly due to egotism — the egotism that brought him to the top. Even so, I would always side with Shaw the Super-man against Chesterton the Common Man, simply because Shaw has transcended to such a remarkable degree all the human romances and emotions which Chesterton swears by.

P.S. To switch from the sublime to the ridiculous; I have just got a letter from Desmond posted in Paris. If I tried to describe their adventures in that car (which seems to have no sides or roof!) you wouldn't believe me. I read that France is going through a severe crisis at present and there are fears of internal collapse. The government is at a loss what emergency measures to take. Obviously they should deport Wilbur and Desmond as a first step, and then plan accordingly.

July 10th 1948

Courtney old lad,

It seems you chose the right year to come over to England. Except for two weeks in May, we have had nothing but wind, cloud, and rain. It is generally admitted that last year's summer was phenomenal. This year we have normal English weather upon us.

I am sure you are right about 'Chrome Yellow'; the idea

177

is borrowed from Peacock — and not very well either. The satirical bits and the parodies (what might be called the Peacockian elements) are the weakest in the book. Huxley is just not a humorist, and his efforts in this direction are insipid and uninspired. Occasionally he rings the bell, but for the most part, because he lacks natural gaiety, his humorous lines are too calculated. One sort of hesitates to laugh because one cannot imagine Huxley himself laughing. Either he thinks life is too serious a matter to be laughed at, or he is afraid of being funny. For if you are going to be funny you must stick your neck out: you must take the risk of your joke falling flat, and yourself looking foolish in consequence. Huxley will not take this risk. He is too dignified. So, like Somerset Maugham, who is better at the game than he is, he remains on the plains of humorous literature with his dignity intact.

Speaking of Maugham, I am going to send you a copy of the 'Writer's Notebook' as a birthday present. I have just finished reading it, and found it very absorbing with the exception of the poetic verbal picture post-cards which I skipped. He is at his best when delivering reflections on Life, and these are in the same vein from his adolescence right up to the present — when suddenly, on the very last page, his guard slips and his life-long agnosticism is confounded. What a pity: it was flawless! Perhaps he felt he must leave a Last Message to mankind. Who knows? Anyway, he delivers his homily on the Nobility of Man, and there it is.

Up to the last page, we have the typical Maugham; smug, absurdly detached, cruelly humorous, who shrugs his shoulders at life with the words: 'Man is born into trouble as the sparks fly upward: that is normal, and we may just as well accept the fact. If we do, we can regard it with that mingling of resignation and humour which is probably our best defence.'

Yes, this is the typical Maugham: the supine sceptic who ignores the partial success of idealists who have ameliorated the lot of mankind. The Maugham who revels in his own detachment; who is continually watching — not only the world, but himself. How cautious he is: how uneasy he feels when tempted to express any positive conviction other than on aesthetics, which he believes to be a study of illusion, in any case. He takes refuge in agnosticism because he cannot bear to feel unsafe, and a positive belief in anything must always be defended. Like Huxley, he lives in constant fear of looking foolish; that is, of looking foolish in the eyes of others, for he does not mind laughing at himself. So, utilizing every ounce of his formidable intelligence, he fortifies his Castle of Doubt, blocking every nook and cranny. 'I know what I am better than anybody,' he seems to say, 'so nobody can make clever remarks about me!'

It is interesting to compare Maugham's attitude to life with Shaw's. He only mentions Shaw once in the Notebook, and you feel he would sooner be describing a Javanese rubber planter. Shaw seems to say, 'I am the only person alive who can see anything clearly, therefore I must live as long as I can, for there is much to be done and no one to replace me.' Maugham seems to say, 'Nobody can see anything clearly except possibly himself. Now that I am satisfied I have explored every part of myself as much as I am able, I am ready to die.' And so he sits, cross-legged, idly turning over the pages of a detective story in his French villa preparing himself for extinction.

Have you heard from Desmond since his return to these shores? If not, it will perhaps surprise you to learn that he has fallen in love, or says he has. He has been hanging round this girl who lives in Nottingham, eating at her home, and sleeping in some old car he has bought. Apparently she is a stage-struck damsel of 19, temperamental, romantic, and effervescent. She won't have anything to do with him unless he can prove that he can support her, so we need not waste any space discussing her, need we?

The truth is that he can no longer stand living with his mother, so he is trying desperately to find a girl who will look after him. As his letters evinced none of the symptoms of being in love at all, I wrote accusing him bluntly of trying to convince himself that he was in love with this girl and wanted to marry her in order to provide himself with some incentive for living. He replied that I was "probably right"! I think it is very weak-minded of him, though I sympathize with him to a great extent. Like me, he hasn't the strength to put his back into Life and 'make good', so he must try to find someone to look after him now that he can no longer live with his mother. In my view, he would do better to emulate Wilbur and find a Phyllis, rather than a young beauty who would look upon him as a husband and not a pet.

He has been drifting about living in boarding houses, and says he is going to find a flat in Town. He had a job in a radio shop for three days but was fired. No news of Wilbur.

P.S. I am delighted that you liked the caricature in 'Music Parade' (Beecham looking for a good tune!). It must be many years since I received such unreserved praise from you. And for a drawing.

Sunday, September 5th 1948

Courtney old oyster,

I have been expecting to hear from you for some weeks but no word. I take it you are either struggling with your soul, playing chess, or re-reading the biography of R. E. Lee. You must not expect me to write to you if I cannot expect a reply because the motivating force behind all my letters to you has always been your replies. I never wrote more than a conventional note to either Vere or Wilbur because I knew that no matter how painstaking I was, I would only receive a cursory comment in return, and might not even get that. The moral of all this is that it takes two to tango.

A wire from Wilbur came Thursday, August 19th, saying: 'Probably arrive within 24 hours. Bringing debt and Desmond.' (He owes me £10). I replied as follows: 'You can't drop in on us like this. Mother says most inconvenient. Anyway prefer you and Desmond separately. Write me a letter.'

180

This retort would be sufficient to rebuff an ordinary person but, as I anticipated, it had no effect on the London Terror. On Friday night they phoned from Chester, announcing that they had run out of petrol having taken two days to travel from London. This was because they were running the car on white spirit, and could not exceed 25 m.p.h. Wilbur said they had spent half the day being towed all round Birmingham trying to start the engine. In short, a typical Wilbur–Desmond performance!

Understandably, Mother expressed annoyance at this sudden advent of uninvited guests, but managed to provide for them when they arrived by bus the next morning. They borrowed a coupon from Peter, and tossed a coin to see who was to go back to Chester for the car, Desmond's somewhat battered Hillman. Wilbur won and Desmond went back for it. Wilbur stayed the night and left by train for London the Sunday morning, leaving Desmond behind with his useless car.

I had imagined that the inspiration for this escapade had been Wilbur's; in fact, it was Desmond's. Feeling bored with life and in need of a long motor drive, he had suggested to Wilbur that they should descend on Broad Leas as I was the only person he knew who lived the required distance away. The snag was that he had used all his petrol coupons. However, Wilbur was in touch with a spiv, and Desmond had — somewhat rashly — telegraphed six pounds to Wilbur for the purpose of obtaining some of the blackmarket variety. However, when he went to see Wilbur to collect the coupons, he learnt that the spiv had not so far produced the goods. They tracked the man to some sleazy cinema, and Wilbur with his usual flourish arranged for an 'urgent' message to be flashed onto the screen. At this, the gentleman hurriedly emerged, but of course it was all to no avail as he hadn't got any coupons.

Impasse! No coupons — no mad dash to the north of England. But Desmond was in no mood to be thwarted; in fact, by now they were both keyed up for the trip. So although they did not have enough petrol to get here and none at all for the return journey, they set out having topped up the tank with white spirit.

When Wilbur left here on the 22nd, the arrangement was that he would contact his spiv and post the coupons as soon as he reached London. Until he did so Desmond was stranded at Broad Leas. On Tuesday came a letter saying the spiv was 'out' but that Wilbur would soon have the coupons. Then on Wednesday came a telegram saying 'Expect your underwear presently.' It came by phone and Mother took the call. I was listening on the extension, and she said, "Oh! Thank you" to the operator, and put down the receiver in some confusion.

The end of the week came but the coupons did not arrive. And no word from Wilbur. Desmond sent a reply pre-paid telegram but there was no response. It looked as if he was stuck with us until the new ration book started in December. As each day went by he grew more restless. His conversation became completely dominated by the subject of petrol — and how to get it? To cut a long story short, he borrowed five gallons from a local garage with Mother as security and filled up the rest of his tank with white spirit.

He reached London the same day (he now has a flat, by the way) with two gallons still left in the tank. He at once phoned Wilbur. Phyllis took the call and told him Wilbur was down in Cornwall; but she insisted that he had posted the coupons up here as soon as he had got Desmond's telegram. Presumably they had been stolen in transit. What remains unexplained is why Wilbur did not avail himself of the pre-paid reply to Desmond's telegram if he had been intending to dispatch the coupons at once.

Mother wrote to Desmond imparting some well-meant maternal advice to the old boy, and received a ten page reply which I can only describe as 'vintage Desmond'.

"Far from needing to cultivate a suspicious attitude," he wrote, "I already have this undesirable quality. I am always suspicious of people's motives, so occasionally, in an attempt to convince myself I am not suspicious, I do idiotic things like lending Wilbur money without a receipt or an

I.O.U. I blindly believe all he tells me in the dim hope that my suspicions will prove unjustified. Very occasionally they do.

"It is horrible always being suspicious of everybody, and worse still knowing that your suspicions are nearly always justified. It is almost as horrible to know (or suspect!) that other people are suspicious of oneself, and worse to realize that their suspicions are also nearly always justified. Consequently, I take a huge delight in proving other people's suspicions about myself to be groundless. I don't admit to myself that the only reason their suspicions are proved groundless is because I enjoy the discomfiture I give them by making them conscious of their unjustified suspicions, and not because I am innately honest. . .

". . .Unfortunately, I sympathize and share with Wilbur's attitude to such an extent that I find it impossible to censure him."

It is a beautiful piece of reasoning, and that, in my opinion, is where it falls down. The whole thing is intellectual humbug! Unlike you, Desmond rarely pays any attention to the part 'temperament' plays in influencing one's judgements and actions. He is a rationalist, and seeks to explain his actions entirely on rational grounds. You have just read his proof that he is not innately honest, and I don't think I have ever met a more innately honest person than Desmond. The real reason why he trusted Wilbur as far as he did was — as anybody can see — he could not resist what appeared to be a chance of getting hold of some precious petrol coupons. He knew it was risky but he succeeded in convincing himself that the risk was negligible because he wanted the coupons so badly. A heroin addict would behave in the same way in order to get the stuff. In short, there was nothing 'rational' about Desmond's decision at all.

A *bon mot* from Mother seems to support this analysis. "He needs looking after, and is really a nice boy although he pretends he isn't."

Wilbur did pay me back £3, but God-knows how much he owes Desmond who had put fifty into the car that Wilbur smashed up in France. Wilbur is learning French with a view to getting a job in a Swiss hotel and reading Maupassant in the original.




Courtney old lad,

Some bad news. It seems your pessimistic prognostications regarding the Square Peg Club have been fulfilled. For all practical purposes it is now disbanded.

I have just received a long letter from Desmond. As you know, he is living in a rented flat in London, and prepares all his own meals and does his own washing and cleaning. Apparently he has no time for anything else as he says he is very slow at doing things. He is lonely, but he has a girl friend. This new one works at an illegitimate baby clinic, and judging from what he says, I don't think there is much chance that he might augment the ranks.

Anyway, he went away to visit his mother and Monica last week-end, and when he got back he found that the door of his flat had been damaged. Wilbur had tried to break in. I should explain that since he left Phyllis (to prove to himself that he is self-sufficient) Wilbur had moved into Desmond's flat for a while, and had brought some furnishings with him. But he was not, in fact, trying to regain possession of these. He was, to quote Desmond, "out for my blood" having just been released from jail where he had been languishing due to Desmond's failure to put up £30 for bail. (The charges: the usual motoring offences plus alimony defalcations.) Although he owed Desmond a sum of money, Wilbur considered he should have put up the bail, and more or less held him responsible for his incarceration.

Anyway, Wilbur had been interrupted before he could break the door down, and Desmond returned to find everything in order. He immediately put Wilbur's belongings into the passage in case he returned — keeping some

curtains with which to raise the money Wilbur owed him —
and waited for him.

Wilbur came round the next morning, very angry and
spoiling for a fight. He gave Desmond a black eye, and left
threatening vengeance and saying he was going to set thugs
onto him. Desmond, of course, took this with his usual
aplomb. He says that the thought of those thugs lying in wait
for him at night has given his life new meaning providing
him with just the stimulus he needs. He is also very proud of
his black eye which is the first one he has ever had. He seems
fonder of Wilbur than ever, but he says he can no longer
afford to have him as a friend.

It is Wilbur I feel sorry for. A jail-bird, dogged by the
police with no Phyllis to protect him, he seems to be headed
for a sticky end. Desmond says he can no longer cope with his
financial worries and has reached the point where he has
ceased to make the attempt. He has lost his self-respect.
Desmond relates how Wilbur's landlady phones him up in
despair, describing how Wilbur comes in after midnight,
leaves his room like a pig-sty, burns the electric stove all day,
uses up all the hot water, and brow-beats her so much that
now she locks her door whenever he is about. She has
complained to the police who have promised to have him
evicted.

What can I say about all this, old lad? It is all very sad.
Deolali seems a long long way away now. . .


September 26th 1974

Dear Courtney,

The envelope arrived while I was away from the flat.
Somehow the postman pushed it through the letter-box. It's
amazing how you've kept the letters all these years: I don't
think there is one missing. But if I had known you were going
to, I'd have written 'em on stouter paper. They look like the
Dead Sea Scrolls.

185

I've read them all — in order, and it's quite a human document. The main thing I didn't realize then — and only time and experience can teach this — is that the Services are only the world in uniform, and if you are a hopeless misfit there, you will be just as much a misfit in the world outside. (I never found that mythical 'niche' I was always looking for.) This is what you cannot know at nineteen when the horizon is miles away and you are full of hope. Though even then I had the insight to found the Square Peg Club.

I also read the Carbacker story. I like the plot — your effort, I believe. But the rococo style is outrageous! It's so absurd that at last I am able to come to a final definitive conclusion on our momentous quarrel. Remember? Should Miss Bayliss smoke the cigar? Thirty years ago I said 'yes'. And now, after due cogitation and, I feel, from a standpoint of objective detachment, I say 'yes' again! The whole thing is so utterly absurd, straight out of Lewis Carroll, that the spectacle of Miss B. smoking a cigar ought to pass almost unnoticed.

Au rev,

Graham

P.S. Hope you are well and all that.

# APPENDIX

These are the two short-stories mentioned in the early letters.

This multilated version of the Sponge King story appeared, somewhat incongruously, in a 1953 children's annual published by Daily Mirror Newspapers Ltd. with illustrations by Mervyn Wilson. The war-time ending and setting — as given here — had been altered.

The Carbacker story, also reduced here from its flowery original, has not been in print before.

I suppose today Cosmo and Hank would be classed as 'mentally disturbed' with 'behaviour difficulties'.

# The Decline and Fall of Cicero

The library of the Aaron Burr High School, Ivoria, Virginia, was normally a salubrious place devoted to reading, writing, and thinking. However, on this particular afternoon the entire student body plus the faculty (including the Engineer in Charge of the Furnace) had assembled there, with the result that the usual quiescent atmosphere had become a trifle disturbed. The man chiefly responsible for this disturbance was the Principal of the school, one Plimsoll Carbacker P.H.D., who was addressing the gathering in stentorian tones. Mr Carbacker was a large thick-set man who habitually wore a loose tie, rolled up shirt sleeves, and a harassed expression to show he worked hard. He had once been caustically described as '215 pounds of bone and muscle and little else.'

Mr Carbacker had made a joke, which was indicated by his raucous laughter. He beamed affably as he listened to the perfunctory applause, then he mussed up his hair, pulled his tie even looser, and cleared his throat.

"Well, I guess you all know what we're here for," he declared. "So I'll hand over to the lady on my right. . . A big hand now to Mrs Sniklebaum!"

He stood aside clapping loudly, and Mrs Lucius B. Sniklebaum moved sedately forward rather like a Graf Zeppelin heading for its mooring mast. She was clutching a trunk-like alligator handbag, the fastening of which she proceeded to click at odd intervals.

"Boys and girls," she shrilled, smiling winningly. "I won't make a speech as I know you all want to get back to work. . ."

This was good — well up to Mr Carbacker's own comedic standard. He must have thought so too as he was braying like a jackass.

"I expect you all know what's under that cover." She glanced across at a tall apparition draped in a white sheet near the window. "Before my dear husband died, he felt he must bequeath one of his magnificent bronzes to the school;

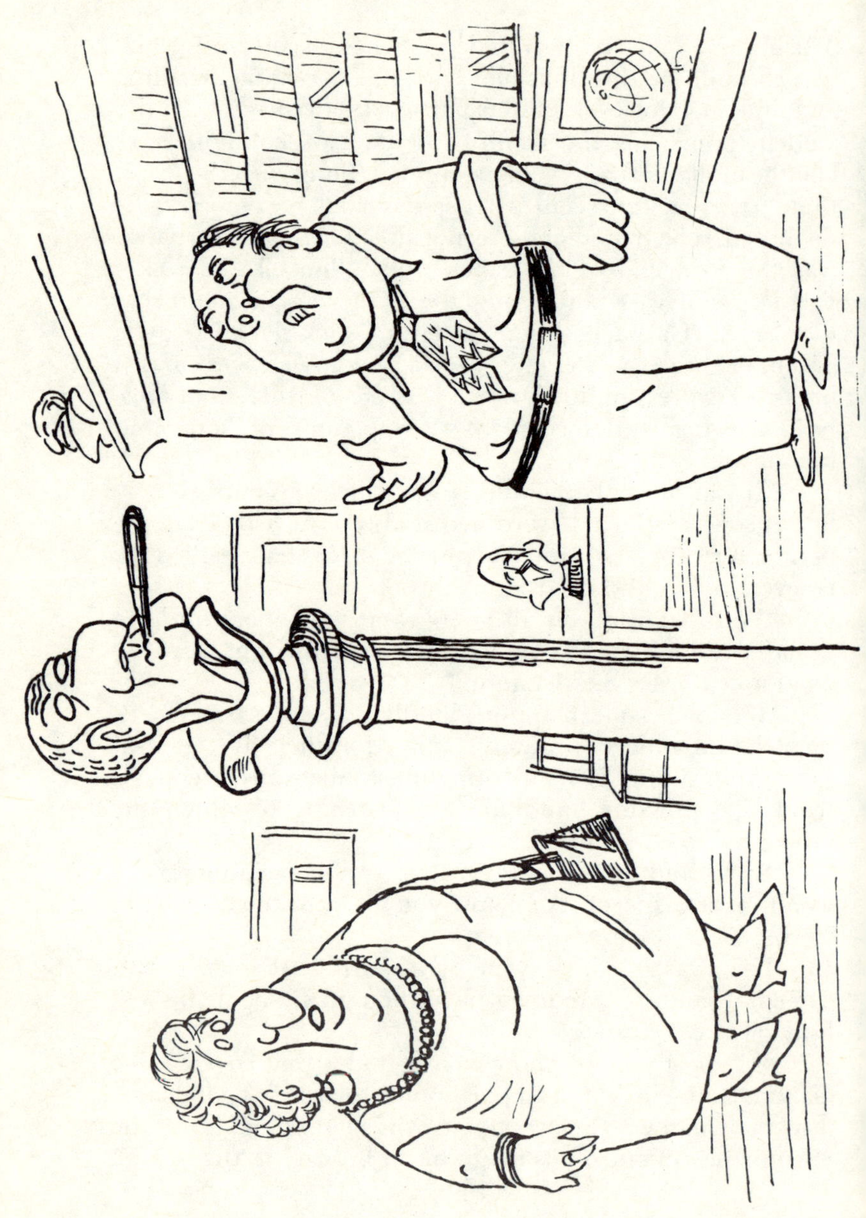

the school where both of us had spent so many happy days, and where — dare I say it — we became sweethearts so long ago. . ."

This brought the house down, and it was several minutes and after a great deal of handbag clicking before Mrs S. was permitted to proceed. The interval had allowed her time to approach the covered bequest.

"I know you must be all tipsy with suspense," she sniggered, grabbing the cord Carbacker was proffering. "So here it is. . . the bust of Cicero!"

She tugged the cord, and the veil dropped.

Marcus Publius Cicero (106–43 B.C.), father of his country, would I am sure, have been impressed by the sculpture that stood revealed to the assembled throng. It was an impressive work of art: the eyes, ears, nose and throat all closely resembled the antiquated features of the 'Opposition to Cataline' fellow. So much so that if Cataline himself had happened to bump into it on a dull day, he would — after first feeling for broken bones — have cried out, "Hiya Marcus!" Although he might have been puzzled by the large cigar inserted between the sculptured lips. Tobacco was not in use in Ancient Rome.

For a moment there was a stunned silence; and it was Carbacker who recovered his wits first. Letting out a bellow like a bull, he roared,

"Who the devil did that?!!"

When the plaster had finished falling from the ceiling, Carbacker strode purposefully to the nearest bookshelf and returned with a heavy volume of the Encyclopaedia Brittanica (BABA–BAXB, to be exact). This he placed on a wooden chair, and having climbed onto it, reached up to grasp the cigar.

Mr Carbacker had never taught Physics: had he done so, he might have been aware that it is impossible for a library chair with Volume BABA–BAXB of the Encyclopaedia Brittanica placed on it to maintain an angle of forty-five degrees for long. As Sir Isaac Newton might have put it: 'What goes up must come down.' And Mr Carbacker, having gone up, now put into practical demonstration the latter part of the theory.

Suddenly he gave a desperate cry, hovered in the air for one breath-taking moment, and then landed on the floor like a paratrooper who had counted to a hundred instead of to ten. The cigar flew out of the window while the bust of Cicero followed Mr Carbacker's example by also committing itself to Newton.

Amidst the ensuing uproar two students at the back of the hall seemed to stand out due to the demonstrative nature of their mirth. One, a tall angular youth whose absurd eye-glass hinted at his English origin: he looked like one of those aristocrats one sometimes sees pictured in the left-wing journals under the caption, ENGLISH DRONES — THEY MUST GO! The other, an American of the same age whose resemblance to Cary Grant was marred by a long neck, big ears, and flat feet. Both lads, however, had one thing in common: a large cigar protruded from each of their top pockets.

As I say, the two lads had been drawing attention to themselves, and it was perhaps for this reason that the eagle eye of Miss Bayliss, Assistant Principal of Aaron Burr and known as Frumpy Phoebe throughout the school, happened to alight upon them. With a cry of triumph she bore down the aisle, and seconds later they were standing before Mr Carbacker.

"Both these boys had these cigars in their pockets, Mr Carbacker," she explained as she handed them over.

Mr Carbacker looked at the cigars, then he glared at the two youths.

"What are your names?" he demanded as the assembly listened in silence.

"Cosmo Darton, sir," said the lanky one affably. "And this is my friend, Hank Prank."

"You're sure about that?" said Carbacker suspiciously.

"Absolutely positive," murmured Cosmo, and then added quickly. "I know what you're thinking, sir. But I assure you that both these cigars are Prince Pinkertons and quite different from the one that's gone out of the window."

"How d'you know that?" barked Carbacker.

"Well, I . . . er," began Cosmo desperately.

"We could see the colour of the band," chipped in Hank.

"You could?"

"Yes, sir. At a guess, I would say it might be an El Rocko Grande."

"It's stuck on a ledge, Mr Carbacker," anounced Miss Bayliss who was leaning rather perilously over the sill.

Mr Carbacker verified this for himself. Then he looked round the hall.

"Where's Riley?" he thundered, and the Engineer in Charge of the Furnace came forward. "Riley. We want a ladder — a long ladder."

Riley looked crestfallen. He had been expecting something of the sort. The ladder, he explained, was being used for tree-lopping and would not be available till the evening.

"In that case," proceeded Mr Carbacker who was never a slow thinker, "the cigar will have to remain where it is for the present. . . Boys, I am going to give you a democratic trial. Being as these two cigars have no bands on them, I shall have to smoke all three to determine whether they are the same. You will both of you be at my office at ten o'clock tomorrow morning."

And at that the court adjourned.

★　★　★　★　★

That night a keen observer, or for that matter a half-blind observer, could have discerned a shadowy figure scaling the walls of the Aaron Burr gymnasium. H. Hank Prank, jr. had not been given the nick-name of Snyder the Spider for nothing.

One of his most amazing gifts was his uncanny ability to see in the dark — or so he had always believed until that moment. Having forced open a window and gained entry to the gymn, he moved forward only to trip over the spring-board, somersault over a 'horse' (a feat he had hitherto failed to accomplish) and land among a heap of dumb-bells. Undaunted he picked himself up, and two minutes later he was outside Mr Carbacker's office.

It should be explained to the reader that the two lads had failed to decide on a plan of action. Obviously the thing to do was to break into Carbacker's office and switch the cigars, but Cosmo had backed out. Hank said he was damned well not going to take the risk on his own, and they had parted with some bitterness. Thinking the matter over, Hank had changed his mind rather than risk expulsion from the school, but he was deeply disappointed in his friend.

He was surprised to find the door to the Principal's office unlocked; surprised and somewhat annoyed as he had been fiddling with a lock-picking tool for ten minutes. Anyway, he had gained access, so he tiptoed noiselessly in, or as noiselessly as anyone with flat feet can tiptoe.

He stood stock still. It was pitch dark, and he felt rather than saw an alien presence in the room. He felt it still more when a hard, and no doubt blunt instrument struck him on the base of the skull, and he fell unconscious to the floor.

It must have been a full recess period before he re-opened his eyes and found himself looking into the blurred visage of Cosmo Darton illuminated by flashlight.

"Where am I?" he groaned.

A pained look glittered across Cosmo's monocle.

"I was hoping for something more original," he remarked. "However, to answer your question, you are in Carbacker's office with your head resting on his brass spittoon."

Hank attempted to speak but Cosmo continued.

"I know what you're thinking, old lad: why am I here when I said I wouldn't come? And I could ask you the same thing, old pin in the shirt. Fact is, I didn't see why both of us should risk it, and I knew I couldn't stop you coming if you knew my intentions. . . How's your head?"

"Have you found the cigars?" retorted Hank eagerly.

"They were inside the ornament as we guessed. I have switched them for a couple of Perfecto-Kingos."

Hank raised himself on one arm and produced a cigar of his own from his pocket.

"Look, Cosmo," he said. "Just to put this thing on a mutual basis, why not swap one of yours for one of mine? Okay. . . Ow, my head!"

Cosmo smiled consolingly.

"All right, old shot in the grouse," he conceded. "Anything to oblige a dying man. Come on: let's get out of here."

★　★　★　★　★

Ten o'clock the next morning once more found the two boys in the office, but this time standing before Mr Carbacker with a grimly silent Frumpy Phoebe in attendance.

"Boys," he said, "I am now going to smoke these cigars; but before I do, Miss Bayliss will testify that this cigar here" — he picked up a somewhat bedraggled object from the desk which looked like a cigar which had had a night out — "is the actual cigar stuck in the bust of Cicero."

"That's right," chimed in Miss Bayliss. "I watched Riley retrieve it from the ledge, and he handed it straight to me."

"As you thought, it is an El Rocco Grande. And if its flavour is the same as these other two, you will be proved guilty," went on Carbacker, snipping off the end and striking a match.

For a few moments he smoked thoughtfully, then he did a surprising thing. He handed it to Miss Bayliss, who beneath the eyes of two of her pupils, actually took a teeny-weeny puff. As Cosmo said afterwards, it was something of a shock and inwardly he reeled a bit at the thought of the fastidious Phoebe Bayliss — a secret cigar smoker.

The ordeal proceeded while Mr Carbacker and his

195

Assistant carefully assessed the flavour of the two other cigars. And then the lads saw his expression change.

"Humff," he said frowning. "I must say they seem to be different."

He glanced at Miss Bayliss who was, it must be admitted, sniffing rather than smoking Cosmo's Perfecto Kingo.

"I agree, Mr Carbacker. The other one is a lot stronger," she said.

"Boys," said the great man uncomfortably. "it seems I owe you an apology. . . We must look elsewhere for the guilty party."

"Apology accepted, sir," cried Cosmo. "May we go?"

Carbacker nodded dejectedly. He was a beaten man.

"I'm confiscating the cigars," he said. "And you can both write out, 'I must not smoke cigars' five hundred times."

Hank paused at the door.

"I'm not sure what make those two are," he remarked inconsequently. "We won them as prizes down at the fairground."

★　★　★　★　★

Once outside the room, the two lads paused, looked at each other inscrutably and then smiled.

"I say, old lad," began Cosmo. "I believe we've both. . ."

He broke off, interrupted by the sound of two sharp explosions from within the sanctum.

"I believe we have," drawled Hank. "Great minds tend to think alike."

And at that they strode away.

196

# The Case of the Sinister Cylinders

Few people can stand the rigours of a hot summer's day without liquid refreshment of some sort, and Cosmo Darton and H. Hank Prank, jr. were no exceptions. School had recently broken up for the holidays, and the two boys were lazing in deck chairs on a sunny lawn sipping iced ginger ale. Close to Hank's chair was an alto saxophone which occasionally he would seize and commence to play a few moody bars, much to the aggravation of his companion.

Cosmo was a tall lanky specimen of England's future Empire-builders. He wore immaculate cricket flannels which were suspended by a rather loud tie knotted round his waist. He also wore a monocle. The predominant features of Hank's attire were a sweater of the brightest yellow imaginable and a bow tie of identical hue.

The two boys were spending their holidays with Hank's aunt in West Virginia, and they had not taken long to discover that there was little hope of any excitement in the neighbourhood. At first, the novelty of rising at two p.m. and resting until bedtime had been pleasant, but soon it became boring. The need for excitement of some sort became imperative. It was then that they heard of J. J. Jason, the Sponge King.

J.J. had begun his career with nothing more than the one million dollars inherited from his famous father, 'Jocular Jason' the Oyster Czar. His fortune had doubled in 1910 when he cornered the sponge market, and trebled in 1912 when he monopolized the Amalgamated American Loofah Industry. In no time he became known in all the best sponge circles as the 'Sponge King'. In 1930, he fancied he would like to live in a castle, so he had one built and retired to spend the remainder of his days pursuing his hobby. Every great man has a hobby. Some collect stamps, others make stringed instruments out of toothpicks. Jason was an amateur criminologist.

His interest in crime and detection dated from as far

back as 1911, when having mislaid his collar stud, he found it again, not as you might think by searching for it on his hands and knees, but by bringing his brain to bear upon the question of where he had put it. That was the beginning. The very next day he joined the vast list of subscribers to the Sexton Blake Mystery Library, and on the following Saturday was seen to be wearing a cloth hat and smoking a crooked pipe.

When war broke out, he surrounded his property with a hurricane fence and installed every conceivable burglar alarm that the profits from his sponges could purchase. It was his boast that if West Virginia was invaded, his castle would defy attack.

The castle, which was a mile from the home of Hank's aunt, was regarded with a good deal of curiosity by neighbouring inhabitants and with a good deal more by Cosmo and Hank, who had been toying with the possibility of piercing the defences.

It was night time, and silence had descended upon the castle. The Sponge King was asleep but not, as might be surmised, in his bed. He was reclining in a spacious leather arm-chair in his study with his feet propped up on a footstool.

He had been reading *The Corpse in the Copse*, the author of which states in his preface that, upon reaching page 196, the reader should know who dumped the corpse in the copse, when he dumped it, and how he dumped it. Jason knew the answer to these questions, and a lot more, before turning page 33. The diabolical ingenuity of the criminal had completely failed to deceive him. To J.J. it was perfectly obvious that the corpse was never in the copse at all, but was hanging all the while in a tree upside-down, so that when the discoverer came along and tripped over a hidden wire, which released a hidden spring, which released the corpse (which, incidentaly, was still alive and kicking, and

198

which fell into the copse and broke its neck), the police would think its demise was recent, thus giving the murderer a fool-proof alibi, who by this time had taken a plane to Syracuse where he was busily cooking his mother's breakfast. The plot revealed, the great man slept.

Suddenly sixty-nine alarm bells burst into song. It was a disturbing sound, and J.J. leapt out of his chair. In a flash he had summed up the situation. Somewhere there was an intruder. Hastily, he pulled on his shoes and switched off the light, and there was a gleam in his steely grey eyes as he did so.

At about the same time, two young gentlemen were having a damp argument a few hundred yards away. I say damp, as nobody who is standing in four feet of Mr. Jason's private lake can be truly defined as dry.

"I say! I've just gone and tripped over an eel!" remarked Cosmo pensively.

"If you fondly imagine it's an eel," retorted Hank, "who do you suggest is ringing those bells — Mr. Jason or my Aunt Alice?"

"Good Lord! You don't think he's got trip-wires in the lake, do you?"

"Undoubtedly. The efficiency of Jason is unsurpassed. You know," he went on, and for once there was a note of seriousness in Hank's voice, "I always had my doubts about this fruity idea of yours. Just after crawling through the drainpipe, I had a feeling our luck wouldn't hold."

★　★　★　★　★

Leaving dripping tracks, Cosmo approached the boat-house which stood at the foot of the steep wooded hill leading to the castle. On the left of the castle he could faintly discern the stables, within whose extensive walls slept J.J.'s famous bloodhounds, blissfully ignorant of their impending

frisk. For the object of the night's escapade was to let loose the bloodhounds into the grounds. As Cosmo moved forward, a large clock built into one of the battlements chimed eleven-fifteen.

Silently he slid up to the boat-house door and turned the handle. And in doing so he set off a further sixteen alarm bells. Once inside the boat-house, Cosmo was surprised to find not as he expected, boats, but dozens of packing cases — all, he thought, big enough to conceal a body. He saw himself as the exposer of the biggest murder case of the century. 'Millionaire's Mass Murders Unmasked' would be the newspaper headline.

He stalked forward to test the weight of the packing cases. At which point he tripped over a coil of rope, causing one of them to fall bodily to the floor and disgorge its contents. Cosmo bent down and picked up the corpse by the tail. It had never been a nice rat even before it had died and decomposed.

However, the case, besides containing a dead rat, boasted something of considerably greater interest. Dozens of silver cylinders lay scattered at his feet gleaming ominously in the moonlight.

Ten minutes later, Cosmo was waiting outside the boat-house in a dinghy for Hank's return when the throaty roar of fifteen Berkshire-bred bloodhounds going berserk assailed the night air. With a smile, he realized that all was going according to plan.

"Put 'em up!" snapped a voice.

Gripping a sten gun, J. J. Jason advanced out of the shadows, and Cosmo, who had been standing in the stern of the dinghy, overbalanced and fell backwards into the lake with a splash. Ten seconds later, Hank came running for his life down the hillside, hotly pursued by a pack of rapacious-looking bloodhounds that might all have been doubles for the Hound of the Baskervilles. Preferring a cold plunge to being eaten alive, he followed Cosmo and leapt into the lake.

The room into which the bedraggled forms of Cosmo Darton and H. Hank Prank were introduced a few minutes later was spacious. It was also grandiloquently decorated. A black-jack that had once belonged to the American gangster John Dillenger hung against one of the old stone walls. A suit of Al Capone's bullet-proof underwear adorned part of another. Even the solitary sponge, an emblem of J.J.'s earlier days reposing in a glass case on the mantlepiece, sported a gold inscription which read, 'Loofah With Which The Mississippi Mallet Murderer Washed In Death Cell.'

"Well," said J.J. "I think I've got you two guys all wound up."

"Like a ball," Cosmo murmured.

"Before I call the cops, I'll do the square thing. I'll let you into the secret of how I caught you!"

"We know, sir," said Hank.

"Oh," said J.J. disappointed, "and may I ask how you know?"

"We felt the trip-wire," Hank explained.

"Ah! But how did I know *where* you were?" said the Sponge King, complacently wagging his finger. "I would say that you came from the east shore of the lake, striking a wire near the opposite side. Am I right?"

He leaned back to enjoy the cries of amazement, but as these were not forthcoming, continued:

"The mud on your feet confirms this. You know, the mistake you young whipper-snappers made was in choosing to trespass on the one property in West Virginia that is completely burglar-proof!"

He emphasized this by striking the desk a blow with his fist. At which point it is necessary to inform the reader that on the desk was a row of steel buttons. J.J. could, if he liked, by pressing one of these, open a trap-door in front of his desk, start the egg-whisk going in the kitchen, electrocute the canary, or turn on the taps in the bathroom.* The one he hit electrocuted the canary.

*** Original version. . .** flush the commode on the second floor.

"In future," he continued, "that is — ha-ha — if you have a future, you'll have to be more careful."

He picked up the telephone.

"Just one moment, J.J." said Cosmo nonchalantly. "I think I should tell you that I know all about the boat-house."

The effect of this casual remark on the Sponge King was shattering. The colour drained from his face and the telephone receiver clattered on to the desk from nerveless fingers, opening the trap-door, starting the egg-whisk, and turning on the bathroom taps simultaneously.

"You know all about the. . ."

J.J. gulped. Then slowly, rather painfully perhaps, his mouth broadened into a smile.

"Well, now," he laughed, "I think my little joke has gone far enough! It's just occurred to me that you boys might think I'm in earnest — might think I'm *really* going to call the police! Ha! Ha! Ha! Of course, it's all a joke! I was a boy once myself, you know. . . I like you young fellows! You must both come to supper some time and we'll have a big laugh over this, eh?"

★　★　★　★　★

"I don't get it," said Hank as they swept down the drive on their way home in Jason's big Cadillac. "What did you find in the boat-house, a body or something?"

"Packing cases, old lad," murmured Cosmo with a smile. "Packing cases crammed with tinned food."

"You mean. . .?"

"Precisely. The great J.J. is a Food Horder."

Suddenly the still night air was rent by a far-off howl of anguish.

"Good Lord!" cried Hank. "What was that? It seemed to come from the direction of the lake."

"The boat-house, I should imagine," answered Cosmo gaily. "I expect old J.J. has discovered that I took the trouble to tear off the labels from most of the tins. A jolly night out, what?"

203